**n Adult Approach to
ther Education**

An Adult Approach to Further Education

ALISON WOLF

iea

The Institute of Economic Affairs

First published in Great Britain in 2009 by
The Institute of Economic Affairs
2 Lord North Street
Westminster
London SW1P 3LB
in association with Profile Books Ltd

The mission of the Institute of Economic Affairs is to improve public understanding of the fundamental institutions of a free society, by analysing and expounding the role of markets in solving economic and social problems.

A CIP catalogue record for this book is available from the British Library.

ISBN 978 0 255 36586 4

Many IEA publications are translated into languages other than English or are reprinted. Permission to translate or to reprint should be sought from the Director General at the address above.

Typeset in Stone by MacGuru Ltd
info@macguru.org.uk

Printed and bound in Great Britain by Hobbs the Printers

CONTENTS

The author   9
Foreword   10
Acknowledgements   14
Summary   16
List of figures, tables and boxes   19

1 Introduction   23
Tinkering is not enough   25

2 It really *is* that bad   28
Institutional musical chairs   29
Central direction of expenditures   38
Central direction of content and delivery   44

3 Should we subsidise post-compulsory education and training for individuals? The economic case   55
Human capital, growth and market failure: the
    economic arguments for government funding of post-
    compulsory education and training   58
Summary   73

4 Should we subsidise workplace training? 78
Training 'on the job' 79
Poaching and pay scales 81
Summary 88

5 Employers as educators: the special case of apprenticeship 90
The state and the individual: further education and higher education 94
Governments and employers 97
The importance of workplace experience 102
Summary 104

6 Psychic income and the 'good society': the non-economic case for subsidy 105
The purposes of education 108
The role of government 110
Summary 118

7 England's post-compulsory education and training sector: evaluating current arrangements 120
Summary of the argument so far 120
Individual entitlements 120
The employer's role 121
The government's role 122
The provision of individual entitlements 125
The employer 133
The government 138

8 Government provision for further and adult education – a new model 145

The structure of subsidy programmes 146

The way forward 155

Paying for it all: changing the way government spends money 162

Conclusion 169

References 170

About the IEA 180

THE AUTHOR

Alison Wolf is the Sir Roy Griffiths Professor of Public Sector Management at King's College London, where she directs the MSc in Public Services Policy and Management. She is a visiting professorial fellow at the Institute of Education, University of London, where she previously held a chair in education. She has been a consultant or adviser to various previous incarnations of the Department for Children, Schools and Families and the Department for Business, Innovation and Skills, and to many past and present education quangos, as well as to the OECD, EC and overseas governments, including those of Australia, South Africa and New Zealand. She is currently a member of the Council of the United Nations University and of the International Accounting Education Standards Board, and worked for some years as a policy analyst in the United States government.

Alison Wolf's research interests are in the interface between education and the labour market, and especially in professional, technical and higher education. Her books include *Does Education Matter? Myths about Education and Economic Growth*, and she also writes frequently for the national press. She won the Sam Aaronovitch Memorial Prize in 2008 for a critique of the Leitch report on skills; and the Work Foundation's prize for feature of the year in 2006 for her article (for *Prospect*) on the changing role of elite women in the workplace.

FOREWORD

During the 2001 general election campaign, I remember listening to journalist Daniel Johnson discussing the government's and opposition's counter-claims regarding the provision of public services. Both main parties were campaigning on government-provided services with slogans such as '20,000 more nurses' or '12,000 more teachers' and so on. All discussion of government-provided services was expressed in the form of desires to increase inputs. There was absolutely no enthusiasm whatsoever for discussing how services might be produced to provide greater consumer welfare. Daniel Johnson commented that the UK political parties were behaving like the old Soviet masters who would proclaim that there were 'thousands more tractors' while the people were malnourished. In that general election campaign, it did not even cross the minds of the major political parties that policy on health, education and so on should be oriented towards consumer satisfaction rather than the maximisation of inputs.

Things have moved on a little since 2001 in the political debate surrounding compulsory education (age five to sixteen) and higher education – where undergraduates now pay a considerable part of the cost themselves and enjoy relative freedom. With every reform, however, the further education system looks more and more as if it is designed with no aim in mind other than to meet government targets. There is no attempt to make the consumer of further education sovereign or the providers free to meet the needs of consumers. The results are predictable. As Alison Wolf, who is one of the leading academics in her field, shows, many courses are provided which are supposed to be vocational but which clearly have a negative economic value; the success of policy is judged by the number of qualifications awarded or the number of people attending particular types of courses (regardless of the usefulness of these courses); the opinions and preferences of people using the further education system simply do not enter into policy development; the whole system is centrally planned by a web of quangos that is continually being reorganised.

The extraordinary range of interest groups from which policy must be wrested is perhaps indicated by one of the government's most recent creations, the 'Joint Advisory Committee for Qualifications Approval'. This body determines whether courses and qualifications can be funded and includes representatives of sixteen quangos,[1] including an entirely different body whose purported and official purpose is actually to regulate and approve qualifications.

The dysfunctionality of all this could be illustrated in many ways. As has been noted, the author cites negative returns to many further education courses. She also shows how the amount of money spent on advisory and inspection services within the further education sector is about twelve times the sum spent on higher education. While further education spending rose by over one third in the six years to 2007, there has been a dramatic drop in students. Because the government's targets to providers of further education are so often expressed in terms of the number of

---

1   In fact, two or three of the members are broadly private sector body representatives – the dividing line is sometimes unclear.

qualifications achieved, providers have strong incentives to ensure that as little as possible needs to be learned to obtain a qualification and, as the author says, '[S]tudy after study shows that these qualifications mostly do nothing for people's earnings'.

The author does not attempt to suggest how much money should be spent on further education. She does, however, lay out a general case for some intervention and some government spending to address particular problems that she believes might not be solved by the market alone. Furthermore, Alison Wolf suggests a whole new way of organising further education policy so that any money that is spent is used much more efficiently and so that supply follows genuine demand. The results of current policy are entirely predictable given that providers of further education receive only 7 per cent of their income in the form of fees paid by the people who are supposed to be benefiting.

What should be done? After a lucid but rigorous review of the theory and evidence (from the UK and abroad), the author lays out various approaches. She argues that there is a case for government subsidy to students and a case for government loan guarantees. Though there may be a case for the provision of some support for employers providing apprenticeships (but not on current lines), all other support should be directed through students. The author argues that such a system works well in higher education, despite some faults. Currently the amount of student-directed funding in higher education is nearly thirty times that in further education – not because total spending is larger but because of a completely different logic driving policy.

There are many advantages to the author's proposed approach. Most obviously, students – who are adults, post-eighteen – are the best judges of their own interests. Only students have the specific knowledge about what they need to learn and how the learning is best undertaken. The incentives to educators to provide worthwhile courses would be much stronger. There could also be closer integration between higher and further education if this route were followed.

It should not be thought that further education is a trivial sector in which there is little interest. The provision of further and adult education was once a great private industry – often supported by local government in a relatively benign way. It provided training courses with rigorously certified private qualifications (the names of some of which still roll off the tongue). This system has been bureaucratised and destroyed. Non-university education beyond the age of eighteen should have great value and, if suitably reformed, could do so again. The author is to be congratulated for untangling this complex web and setting out a rational basis for policy.

PHILIP BOOTH

Editorial and Programme Director,
Institute of Economic Affairs
Professor of Insurance and Risk Management,
Sir John Cass Business School, City University
October 2009

ACKNOWLEDGEMENTS

This monograph deals with an area of education policy on which I have worked for many years. While all the conclusions and recommendations are my own responsibility, as are any errors, I have benefited from the advice and insight of very many people who work in further education colleges, private training companies, government departments, industry organisations and quangos. Without their help, and their often trenchant criticisms of current practice, I would have found it impossible to understand the extraordinary system that successive English governments and policymakers have managed to create, and completely impossible to write this volume. I have not attempted to list names, partly because they are so numerous but also because I was told a good number of things in confidence. I would, however, like to express my deep gratitude to everyone who has, over the years, shared information and ideas, argued with me, corrected me, or commented on things I have written.

John Harwood, John Stone and Nick Barr all gave me detailed comments on an earlier draft; and one of John Harwood's suggestions for implementation is central to my recommendations. The views and recommendation expressed here are, however, entirely my own. I would also like to acknowledge a general debt to Nick Barr for his work on higher education funding, which informs much of my own discussion. The clarity and thoroughness with which, over the years, he worked through the arguments for and against public subsidies, student contributions and income-contingent loans are an example to anyone concerned with policy.

Nick Linford was unfailingly helpful in answering my questions about particular wrinkles and peculiarities of funding: any remaining errors are mine. Magdalen Meade helped prepare the figures. The excellent charity They Work for You has made the life of researchers and analysts far simpler by providing a dedicated search engine for parliamentary questions and answers, and I used it intensively.

SUMMARY

- Governments currently spend enormous amounts of money on what sometimes seems to be the 'invisible' sector of further and adult education and skills training.
- In England, over the last decades, this sector has been subject to ever-increasing levels of central planning and control, and constant reorganisation. One recently created addition to the regulatory system for further education is made up of representatives from fourteen other education quangos and two private sector bodies.
- Centrally set qualification targets, rather than student demand, have determined what is taught. Many of the qualifications that government promotes and funds directly have no economic value.
- 'Skills' initiatives have also been the government's main policy for raising productivity growth. This has involved increasing spending on programmes located in employers' premises that are intended to provide free or highly subsidised training in skills of immediate relevance to current production. This money displaces employers' own spending and has been used to cover the cost of formal accreditation of already existing skills.
- Overall, the system demonstrates all the usual defects of central planning and the government's belief that most

adults are unable to make sensible decisions for themselves. A conservative estimate is that £2 billion a year of further education and skills spending – i.e. almost half of total government expenditure in the sector – is wasted, providing no net benefit to individual learners or society at large.

- Although current English policy is profoundly misconceived, there are valid arguments for government spending on post-compulsory education. Individuals may underestimate returns from education and may face difficulties borrowing in the usual credit markets. This will be especially true for poorer adults, who are also likely to be more risk averse.

- Governments can and should address these problems by ensuring that credit is available, to individuals, at low long-term interest rates on an income-contingent basis. In England, this has been the approach taken for young full-time undergraduates, but to date only for them.

- There are no good reasons for governments to provide subsidies to employers for training related to their current activities. There is no empirical evidence showing substantial underinvestment in training by employers. Subsidies to employers – mostly large employers – inevitably discriminate against new and future entrants. The possible exception to this general rule is that employers could be subsidised to provide apprenticeships.

- Further education subsidies should go directly to and through individuals; provision should respond directly to their preferences and choices, not to governments' purchases on their (supposed) behalf.

- For long courses (including degrees, but also higher diplomas, college-based craft training, apprenticeships and general education courses such as A-levels for adults) the current pattern of funding undergraduates provides a good model that can be generalised.

- For 'occasional' learning, such as evening courses, or intensive training sessions, formal course-specific contracts for loans are cumbersome and uneconomic. Transaction costs can be minimised by creating individual learning accounts, operated by a government-guaranteed organisation, from which payments can be made, but only for education and training purposes. Payments into these accounts would trigger government contributions, as happens at present with payments into 'charity accounts' used to make donations to charity.

FIGURES, TABLES AND BOXES

Figure 1a Agencies responsible for the funding and
content of post-compulsory training and
education programmes in England: government
departments, 2006–09   31

Figure 1b Agencies responsible for the funding and content
of post-compulsory education and training
programmes in England: quasi-governmental
bodies (quangos), 2006–09   32

Figure 2a FE and adult enrolments 1996–2005
(all institutions)   36

Figure 2b FE and adult learners funded directly by the
Learning and Skills Council   37

Table 1   JACQA core membership   34
Table 2   Expenditures on advisory and inspection bodies,
core funding: HE versus FE plus 'skills'   37
Table 3   Percentage of adults reporting current or recent
participation in learning by socio-economic class   40
Table 4   Expenditures and projected expenditures on
employer-based training programmes, England,
2006–11   42

Table 5   Government expenditures on student support
           (maintenance and non-fee costs): higher and
           further education, England, 2007–09   129
Table 6   Average returns to Level 1 and 2 vocational
           qualifications in the UK, by gender: full-time
           employees of working age   142
Table 7   Expenditure on post-compulsory education and
           training, 2008/09   164

Box 1   Train to Gain   41
Box 2   Excerpt from 'Qualifications and Credit
           Framework'   46
Box 3   A Train to Gain success?   51
Box 4   Subsidised education and the public good   61
Box 5   Income-contingent loans   66
Box 6   Government misinformation (1)   72
Box 7   Government misinformation (2)   74
Box 8   Apprenticeships in Germany   97
Box 9   Apprenticeships elsewhere   101
Box 10   Adult literacy   116
Box 11   Eligibility for funding   130
Box 12   Train to Gain expenditures   135
Box 13   The Leitch report   141

An Adult Approach to
Further Education

1 INTRODUCTION

This monograph argues for a major reform in our funding and, therefore, our organisation of further and adult education. This sector has always been the most unloved and invisible part of our education system; but has also, in the past, been highly diverse, often excellent, a major avenue of both social mobility and personal development (see Bailey, 2001). Today it is none of these things. It has been laid waste by decades of Soviet-style central planning which have demonstrably failed to fulfil any of the objectives set by government, and destroyed most that was good in the process. Billions of pounds have been and are being spent to no good purpose, and the present system is unreformable in anything approaching its current form.

This monograph sets out the principles for a coherent approach to funding and providing further and adult education, as well as concrete policy proposals. It is important to be clear about exactly what aspect of the education system we are discussing because there is much confusion about this. *'Further and adult education', for these purposes, covers everything that is neither education for under-eighteens, nor based in a designated institution of higher education, normally a university.* There is some activity based in further education (FE) colleges but classified as 'higher' education because of the sort of qualifications to which it leads. This is funded through the same institutions as fund universities (mostly the Higher Education Funding Councils). This monograph does not address FE-based higher education explicitly, but the arguments made here generalise to it. Indeed, they generalise to all forms of post-compulsory education, however labelled, now and in future; and one of the main contentions of this monograph is that we need to think about post-compulsory education in a much more holistic way rather than treating what goes on in universities as completely different from what goes on elsewhere.

The further and adult education sectors are not invisible because they are small-scale. They have, like most parts of the public sector, expanded owing to the government largesse of the last few years. Almost as much is spent on further education and training as on compulsory schooling.[1] Yet further and adult education attract almost no media attention – broadcasters never cover Parliamentary Select Committee hearings on the area, and nor do the vast majority of newspapers. Even in the specialist education press, coverage occupies a small, separate 'Further Education' section, which I suspect no one outside the sector ever reads – except, perhaps, other education journalists.

Ministers with a 'skills' brief talk endlessly about how crucial 'skills' and 'training' are to the country's future (the word education having vanished from the government's vocabulary). Tony Blair, on the other hand, once remarked that, if he buried a declaration of war on Iran inside a speech on skills, no one would ever spot it (see Aaronovitch, 2009). His instincts were, as so often, right.

FE is not used by the young middle class. Traditionally it provides training for craft trades or in discrete skills; provides

---

1   By 2007, government expenditure in the sector was well over £8 billion a year, although a sizeable part of this goes to sixteen-to-eighteen-year olds in full-time education. (Many young people study in FE colleges.)

'second-chance' education for adults who have dropped out of education early; provides evening classes for millions of middle-aged and elderly people; and provides training for small local firms. It has never offered a passport to elite careers, and so no one noticed as it became a test bed for reborn central planning – and living proof that this works no better today than it ever has before.

Adopting the proposals set out below would allow the system to become genuinely 'demand-led'. In other words, what is offered, and taught, would reflect the demands of those who study and learn, pay for and use further and adult education. This sounds like motherhood-and-apple-pie stuff; indeed, the mantra of 'demand-led' provision is on everyone's lips, and proclaimed as current policy by the government. The reality of current provision is utterly different, as Chapter 2 makes clear – but it need not be.

Tinkering is not enough

Comprehensive reform is always expensive and difficult. But changes at the margin will not suffice. I am certainly far from the only person to criticise the current regime. To take just a few recent examples from the current policy debate, the centre-left think tank IPPR has called for reform and argued that 'the system should start with the learner' (see Delorenzi, 2007: 71). From the other side of the political spectrum, Reform criticises the current 'unwieldy maze' and proposes that the government should abandon skill plans and targets (see Haldenby et al., 2008). Demos, the House of Commons Select Committee, NIACE and CfBT Education Trust (Centre for British Teachers) have all issued highly critical reports; and the Campaigning Alliance for Lifelong Learning has been criticising declines in adult education with vigour (House of Commons Education and Skills Committee, 2007; Corney, 2007; Oakley and O'Leary, 2008; Schuller and Watson, 2009). But far too often, analysis of the failures of different bits of a bureaucratic and institutional maze culminates in a list of complicated, specific and non-fundamental reforms which are quite as opaque to 99.9 per cent of the population as is the system under review.

Here, I aim to provide, instead, something which has not (at least to my knowledge) been done: namely to look at the basic, underlying justification for any sort of public spending on this area, and, from this, derive some quite clear *general* recommendations for funding and organisation. If one can reach agreement on these it should be easier to address the specifics in a coherent fashion.

A few preliminary points

Further and adult education are not quite like higher education, but they are far more like it than governments believe. Much of what I will say applies to *all formal education and training which is undertaken after the end of full-time compulsory schooling* because all of it shares common characteristics. It involves activity not just by the individual but by others who are being paid by someone to do the teaching and training. In other words, it applies to everything intended to develop oneself in some way that involves others, incurs formalised costs and payments, and is not obligatory by virtue of one's age. If we thought about post-compulsory education in this integrated way we would, in my opinion, make far less of a mess of the non-university-based part of it.

This is not to argue that there should be no such thing as universities, as distinct institutions, and with some quite distinct policies applied to them. But the common division between 'higher education' and other post-compulsory activities obscures their much more important commonalities. Because many clever and important people care deeply about universities there has, not surprisingly, been far more attempt not only to develop but also to evaluate workable ways of funding and running large university sectors. It is very difficult to get something right, from first principles, first time round. In fact, it is because I have borrowed so much from university experiences that I feel fairly confident that what I propose is not only just but practical.

Second, I should warn readers that I do not believe that everything can be left to the market so that government spending in this field should simply stop. I will be arguing that there are some valid arguments both for government spending and for certain types of government activity, although in both cases they involve a system very different from our current one.

Third, the following pages do not say anything about how much, in total, government should spend. That is and must be a political decision. At present all four constituent parts of the UK spend a relatively large amount on education, and on this type of education, by international standards (see OECD, 2008), although much of it in ways and on types of provision which are difficult to justify – especially in England. To believe, however, that one can reach clear judgements about the exact amount of expenditure in different areas which is 'optimal' for the country is, as I have argued at length elsewhere, a delusional fantasy (Wolf, 2002). What one can do is suggest organisational changes which are almost bound, for any given expenditure level, and on any conceivable combination of preferences and behaviour, to take us somewhere better than we are at present.

2 IT REALLY *IS* THAT BAD

For well over twenty years, and at an ever-accelerating rate, further and adult education have been subjected to comprehensive and unprecedented levels of centralised planning, and to sudden and repeated changes. Detailed, expensive and overlapping bureaucratic control has been imposed on all aspects of people's work, and there has been cavalier destruction of large parts of the sector's historic and popular provision. Current arrangements undermine innovation and make it completely pointless for 'providers' – the government's favoured term – to undertake any sort of long-term thinking.

Since 2006, government has imposed yet another new set of changes in order to create a so-called 'demand-led' set of procedures. The term is unashamedly Orwellian, since the only institution whose 'demand' matters or registers is the government itself. In essence, the last few years follow squarely in the twenty-year tradition[1] of endlessly changing and ever more detailed central

---

1 Current policies can trace their origins back directly to the establishment of the National Council for Vocational Qualifications in 1986, which effectively signalled central government's determination to nationalise vocational qualifications (and, therefore, vocational education; see Wolf, 2001). The 1993 incorporation of colleges, as independent institutions, was a more ambiguous decision, giving colleges freedom from LEAs, and imposing a uniform new funding regime, administered through the Further Education Funding Council (1993–2001). At the same time, the introduction of central validation of qualifications, and use of an 'approved' list of what qualifications could be offered, heralded unprecedented

direction, but with one added twist – namely the provision of large taxpayer-funded subsidies to some of the largest employers in the land.

As this chapter explains, further and adult education, including apprenticeships,[2] are subjected to detailed regulation and oversight in three different areas:

1. the institutions that exist, including regulators and advisory bodies;
2. how much money goes to each category of expenditure, including the type and level of course;
3. what exactly is taught and assessed.

The result is an organisational cat's cradle, and a regime of 'hyper-accountability'[3] to government plus non-responsiveness to either the labour market or to individual learners' demands.

Institutional musical chairs

One of the most striking aspects of current policy is its addiction to continual, and ever more complex, institutional reorganisation.

central control over what was taught. This increased greatly with the introduction of the Learning and Skills Council, which plans provision centrally.

2 Apprenticeships have been nationalised and transformed over the last fifteen years and are in most respects the direct successor of the youth training programmes launched during the 1980s at a time of very high youth unemployment. As such they are largely run by professional training companies. The content of an apprenticeship is specified in detail by one or other 'Sector Skills Council' (SSC), government-sponsored and funded bodies which sometimes incorporate old-established employer and trade bodies but are more usually recently created institutions which rely entirely on government funding. SSCs are meant to boost skills in their prescribed area of the economy: see Chapter 5 below.

3 The term is Warwick Mansell's (Mansell, 2007).

This now extends even to departmental level. When the Department for Education and Skills was split in 2007, the sector found itself straddling two departments, DIUS (Department for Innovation, Universities and Skills) and DCSF (Department for Children, Schools and Families). Eighteen months later, DIUS vanished as abruptly as it had arrived, folded into a new departmental empire created (no doubt briefly) for Lord Mandelson: namely DBIS – the Department for Business, Innovation and Skills. But the DCSF, and dual departmental control, continue.

Figure 1a shows the number of government departments that have had direct involvement in the sector in the last few years; and the degree to which these departments have been subject to major internal upheavals. Overlapping jurisdictions and recurrent reorganisation at this level are enough in themselves to make coherent and effective policymaking near-impossible. The upheavals at central government level, expensive and disruptive though they clearly are, are however small-scale and well spaced out compared with those that have been and continue to be visited on the sector by constant changes in, and proliferation of, quangos and inspectorates.

Figure 1b sets out some – only some – of the relevant institutional changes that have occurred in the last four years alone among official bodies, funding agencies, inspectorates and other quangos with a major, direct role in how this sector is run. Many bodies and programmes from the two decades before are not only gone but totally forgotten, their acronyms bemusing even to those of us who have been observing, or working in, the sector for years: FEU, BEC, TOPS, ILBs, NACETT and even the once mighty MSC.[4]

---

4   The MSC was the Manpower Services Commission, a huge quango which ran programmes not only at post-compulsory level but also in schools.

Figure 1a **Agencies responsible for the funding and content of post-compulsory training and education programmes in England: government departments, 2006–09**

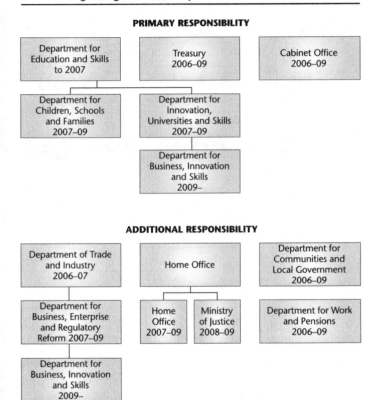

PRIMARY RESPONSIBILITY

Department for Education and Skills to 2007

Treasury 2006–09

Cabinet Office 2006–09

Department for Children, Schools and Families 2007–09

Department for Innovation, Universities and Skills 2007–09

Department for Business, Innovation and Skills 2009–

ADDITIONAL RESPONSIBILITY

Department of Trade and Industry 2006–07

Home Office

Department for Communities and Local Government 2006–09

Department for Business, Enterprise and Regulatory Reform 2007–09

Home Office 2007–09

Ministry of Justice 2008–09

Department for Work and Pensions 2006–09

Department for Business, Innovation and Skills 2009–

Figure 1b demonstrates how short the life of many of these institutions can be. It also demonstrates that their total number has grown steadily, even in this very short period.

This continual reorganisation involves enormous costs. Any

Figure 1b **Agencies responsible for the funding and content of post-compulsory education and training programmes in England: quasi-governmental bodies (quangos), 2006–09**

	2006	2007	2008	2009
Local Education Authorities				
Higher Education Funding Council England				
Quality Assurance Agency				
Regional Development Agencies				
Office for Standards in Education, Children's Services and Skills				
Sector Skills Councils				
Learning & Skills Council				
Qualification & Curriculum Authority				
Sector Skills Development Agency				
Adult Learning Inspectorate				
Learning & Skills Development Agency				
Skills & Employment Boards				
Quality Improvement Agency				
Learning & Skills Network				
Office of the Qualifications & Examinations Regulator				
UK Commission for Employment & Skills				
Joint Advisory Committee for Qualifications Approval				
Skills Funding Agency				
National Apprenticeship Service				
Young People's Learning Agency				
Qualifications and Curriculum Development Agency				

Exists/active   Abolished/closing   Not yet created

new organisation will hire staff, redeploy staff, pay staff to take voluntary redundancy and so on. They will commission letterheads and logos, move offices, issue glossy literature, send highly paid employees on fact-finding missions and to briefings and then to repeated KIT ('Keep-in-touch') meetings with central government bureaucracies and all the other organisations on their horizon.

But these direct costs are only a small part of the total. New oversight organisations impose new requests, responsibilities and therefore major direct costs on the providers of education and training. The latter have not only to work out what the new requirements are, and often re-engineer their own internal bureaucracies and staffing accordingly, but also to dismantle other systems which they have just developed for the previous regime. And because reorganisation is so constant, and information always out of date and subject to imminent change, this behaviour also creates enormous barriers to clear decision-making and understanding, with all the inefficiencies this implies both for providers of education and would-be learners.

What all recent changes have in common is that they promote and institutionalise central government's control over the detailed, day-to-day operations of further and adult education provision. This has been more marked in this sector than it has been for schools and universities but it reflects, in extreme measure, a strong and increasingly dominant strain in education policy generally.[5] This is perfectly illustrated by the most recent institutional innovation (at the time of writing). In 2008, the government announced the creation of a new 'independent regulator of qualifications and tests', to be set up outside Whitehall to regulate and approve qualifications. Official letters and ministerial pronouncements emphasised that 'Ofqual' was indeed to be a 'credible, authoritative and independent voice', not 'part of the delivery chain' for government,[6] and with a remit for schools as well as further and adult education. Legislation is currently establishing it on these lines.

5   Policy under the Tory governments combined greater centralisation in some areas with greater freedom in others (notably for schools and colleges), and New Labour also, under Blair, promoted 'academies': schools with greater freedom and autonomy than the mainstream. Recently, there have been moves to diminish academies' autonomy.

6   Correspondence between Kathleen Tattersall, chair of Ofqual, and Ed Balls, Secretary of State, DCSF: published by Balls, 16 May 2008.

Table 1 **JACQA core membership**

QCDA/QCDA (joint chair)	Association of Learning Providers (ALP)
LSC/YPLA (joint chair)	British Chambers of Commerce (BCC)
Local Government Association (LGA)	National Bureau for Students with Disabilities (SKILL)
UK Commission for Employment and Skills (UKCES)	Department for Children, Schools and Families*
Workforce Agreement Monitoring Group (WAMG)	Department for Innovation, Universities and Skills*
Higher Education Funding Council for England (HEFCE)	Office of the Qualifications and Examinations Regulator (Ofqual)*
Association of Colleges (AoC)	Department for Children, Education, Lifelong Learning and Skills (DCELLS, Wales)*
The Alliance of Sector Skills Councils (TASSC)	Council for the Curriculum, Examinations and Assessment (CCEA, Northern Ireland)*

* Observer status

Source: DCSF, 'JACQA: Frequently Asked Questions'[7]

A truly independent regulator would, of course, be free to approve qualifications that were not the government's favourites, and disapprove others that were. Long before the legislation was even passed, central departments moved to retake control of their planned education economy. Ofqual, it turns out, can regulate as it wishes; but whether or not something is actually funded, and so offered in public provision, will be decided by something else. This is JACQA, the 'Joint Advisory Committee for Qualifications Approval': a non-statutory body, centrally controlled, whose

7   http://www.dcsf.gov.uk/14-19/index.cfm?go=site.home&sid=3&pid=452&lid=545&ctype=FAQ&ptype=single

membership, shown in Table 1, also provides a snapshot of 2009 'quango-land'.

Although it is completely impossible to calculate the total costs of these bodies, the detailed regulation and oversight that characterise adult and further education mean that its quangos and governmental advisory bodies are demonstrably far more expensive than those for higher education, which serves the same post-compulsory population. As a proportion of funds disbursed, the Learning and Skills Council (soon to be replaced by several new and separate quangos: see Figure 1b) spends approximately ten times as much on administration as does the Higher Education Funding Council.[8] This is not because LSC staff are incompetent but because of government departments' involvement in the smallest, day-by-day decisions made by the LSC, with the details of accounting and audit procedures travelling up to the desk of the Secretary of State himself.[9] Micro-management involves major costs within Whitehall as well: college sector observers have estimated that, in 2008/09, 300 civil servants in central government were involved full-time in oversight, monitoring and general second-guessing of the decisions made by the 'skills' sector's supposedly autonomous agencies. Meanwhile, as Table 2 demonstrates, the inspection costs for the sector far outpace those for higher education.

As noted above, there have been large increases in total

---

8   Calculated as an average of expenditures for 2002–07, using information on costs provided by Bill Rammell, MP, in reply to a parliamentary question from Boris Johnson, MP; Hansard, column 200607/070903.

9   Alan Johnson, for example, when Secretary of State for Education, personally reversed changes by the LSC which would have simplified the claims procedure for FE colleges, and the level of detailed documentation and expenditure evidence required (source: personal communication).

Figure 2a **FE and adult enrolments 1996–2005 (all institutions)**
'000s

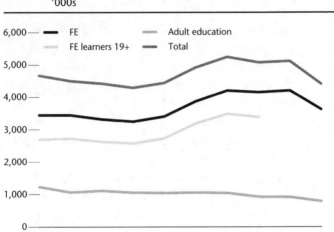

Note: Between 2003 and 2005, published statistics for all learners ceased to provide separate numbers by age group. After 2005, comparable figures for all FE and adult enrolments are not available.
Sources: FEFC Student Statistics; LSC Statistical First Releases (Learner Numbers)

spending since 1997, just as there have in other parts of the public sector. In constant purchasing power terms, spending on FE and workplace training rose from £6.2 billion to £8.6 billion between 2001 and 2007. And yet, as Figures 2a and 2b indicate, *the number of adult students in FE has fallen quite dramatically in the last few years*, compared with major increases in the decade before.

This occurred primarily because central government took a more and more direct role in deciding what sort of courses could be offered (and where they could be offered), and in prioritising certain types of learner, as discussed below. Indeed, the government's own projections are for further declines in the numbers of

Figure 2b **FE and adult learners funded directly by the Learning and Skills Council**
'000s

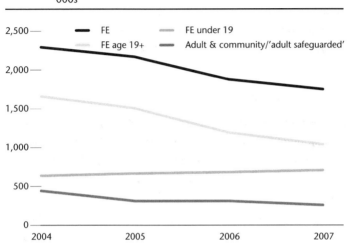

Note: Comparable figures are not available after 2007, when published statistics on FE and skills (currently provided by 'The Data Service' rather than by the LSC or any government department) ceased to differentiate between learners by institutional type/place of learning. Data series on learner numbers and characteristics that go beyond 2007 are effectively impossible to construct at present.
Source: LSC Statistical First Releases

Table 2 **Expenditures on advisory and inspection bodies, core funding: HE versus FE plus 'skills'**

	HE, £millions	FE + skills, £millions
2003/04	2.30	36.97
2004/05	4.55	39.44
2005/06	4.62	39.33
2006/07	3.52	41.82

Note: These sums relate to direct activities and exclude money reallocated to other bodies.

adults enrolled in further education, from the 1.7 million in 2007 to 1.3 million in 2010.[10] The costs of endless reorganisation must nonetheless have contributed to what has been, in recent years, a dismal productivity record in terms of the number of learners who can be served for a given level of expenditure.

Central direction of expenditures

The last decade has been a period of tighter and tighter central regulation of the sorts of provision that will be funded, for which types of student, and in which institutions. As in other parts of government, funding decisions are driven primarily by a Public Service Agreement between a spending department (successively, in the last decade, DfEE, DfES, DIUS, DBIS) and the Treasury. In the present case, the department undertakes to ensure that a given number of people obtain qualifications within a specified time period. These targets are fed through to the quangos which disburse funding (in succession, since 1997, the FEFC and TECs; the LSC; and, shortly, the YPLA and SFA: see Figure 1b above). They in turn sign contracts with colleges and private training providers which undertake to deliver a specified number of particular types of qualification (*not* courses) that contribute towards the targets.[11]

One increasingly visible result is that many of the courses and classes that adult learners took have been withdrawn, not because

---

10 Figures are for learners funded through 'Adult Learner Responsive' funding (*sic*). Information provided by Bill Rammell, MP, in response to a parliamentary question, 1 April 2008; Hansard, column 851W/852W.

11 Although some provision may be funded which does not lead to qualifications, or to qualifications that are not high-priority in terms of central PSA-set targets, the proportion of funding allocated specifically to target-linked qualifications has increased steadily since 1997: see Fletcher and Perry (2008) and Linford (2008).

no one wanted to take them but because they lost funding. The funding has been diverted in large part to longer, full-time courses, meaning that fewer students can be enrolled for given levels of funding. More generally, as discussed further below, money has been withdrawn progressively from college-based courses and funnelled into activity on employers' premises. Any courses that do not lead to a formal vocational qualification have also been progressively discontinued.

As adult education courses have disappeared from state-subsidised institutions, middle-class learners have often been able to find substitutes, notably in the 'self-help' structures of the University of the Third Age. This has not been the case for other groups. Table 3 charts trends in participation in learning, with responses covering participation in publicly funded but also other provision, using data for the annual participation survey carried out by NIACE (National Institute for Adult and Continuing Education). It shows that for 'C1' learners – skilled working-class – participation levels are now lower than they were in 1996.

The central planning of further and adult education is based on a blind faith that increasing the volume of education and training has a direct and positive effect on economic growth,[12] and a conviction – which is discussed and accepted to some extent in Chapter 3 – that in an unregulated market there will always be serious market failure in the provision of education and training. These are coupled with a conviction that the only forms of education and training that justify government subsidy are those that contribute directly to economic productivity – that we 'educate to grow to educate to grow to educate to grow'. The

---

12 For counter-arguments, see Pritchett (2001), Shackleton (1992), Wolf (2002, 2004).

Table 3 **Percentage of adults reporting current or recent participation in learning by socio-economic class**

	1996 per cent participating	2002 per cent participating	2008 per cent participating
Total sample	40	42	38
AB	53	60	51
C1	52	54	46
C2	33	37	33
DE	26	25	26
Weighted base	4,775	5,885	4,932

Source: Adapted from Aldridge and Tuckett (2008: Table 6)

policies developed from these principles also evince (and demand) total confidence in the government's own ability to fine-tune the system and offset 'market failure' in a consistent and effective way. It is this constellation of beliefs which has led to the running down of adult education, and the increasing concentration of expenditure on tightly defined programmes that promote 'skills'.

The most important recent initiative is a very large programme called 'Train to Gain' (see Box 1), which absorbs almost a third of the budget for education and training for those over eighteen and is projected to absorb larger proportions still in coming years. Its name encapsulates the assumptions and objectives of current policy and, although it is just the latest in a string of policies and programmes, it is also the largest and most ambitious to date. Train to Gain money is strictly for use in the workplace and can only be used to 'deliver' a certain subset of qualifications from an approved list: all those on the list have gone through a long approval process run by government quangos, and have been assigned a 'level' in the 'National Qualifications Framework'. Meanwhile, provision within colleges is also restricted,

Box 1 Train to Gain

'Train to Gain' is a flagship policy for Gordon Brown's government, building on a programme called 'Employer Training Pilots', which he instituted while Chancellor of the Exchequer and which was run from the Treasury, independently of the (then) Department for Education and Skills. It offers employers free training and accreditation in the workplace. ETPs also, in some areas, offered money to replace wages when employees took time off. The rationale is the classic 'market failure' argument, namely that firms will train at sub-optimal levels because they cannot capture the benefits of their training expenditures (see also Chapter 3).

Train to Gain was and is scheduled to absorb ever-increasing proportions of the post-sixteen education and training budget. Table 4 below shows the government's detailed projected expenditure levels and patterns, as set out in its remit letters to the Learning and Skills Council, which (currently) distributes money and is responsible for 'delivering' the qualifications and numbers set out in the Public Service Agreements.

with more and more funding tied to contracts for qualifications; more and more restriction on the type of qualification that can be offered; and more and more emphasis on particular 'priority' vocational areas, decided at national level rather than with respect to local labour markets.

Table 4 **Expenditures and projected expenditures on employer-based training programmes, England, 2006–11**

	2006/07	2007/08	2008/09	2009/10	2010/11
	£m	£m	£m	£m	£m
Train to Gain	283	521	657	777	1,023
Employer-based NVQs	269	194	208	214	231
Employer-based expenditures: as percentage of all projected adult expenditure (excludes apprenticeship)	16.2	25.6	31.6	33.1	38.4

Source: LSC Grant letters 2007/08 and 2008/09 (DCFS). (These are used to indicate government policy and intentions, though note that the LSC 2008/09 annual report indicates both a very substantial underspend for 2007/08 and higher expenditures for 2008/09)

Spending the money, however, proved to be unexpectedly difficult. The Train to Gain budget was underspent by £100 million (35 per cent) in 2006/07 and by £207 million (40 per cent) in 2007/08. This occurred even though a good deal of the money that was spent did not go to training 'providers' at all, but on large contracts to 'brokers' whose main task is to contact employers and tell them about the glories of the programme. (Brokers' contracts are 'performance related', but what is counted is simply the number of employer contacts logged, not the numbers of people who actually train as a result.) In 2006/07, 8 per cent of the total Train to Gain budget, and 14 per cent of the amount actually spent, was allocated to broker contracts, while in 2007/08 £38.6 million – 8 per cent of the total budget and 12 per cent of the amount actually spent – was spent on brokers' contracts: fourteen organisations were involved, giving an average of £2.76 million each.[13]

Ministers have appeared both bemused and angry at the underspend. In June 2008, for example, John Denham, the then secretary of state in England for (among other things) 'skills', complained to the TUC that 'some employers are failing not only to spend their own money on staff training – but also failing to spend ours as well. This represents a missed opportunity for businesses. And a missed opportunity for those who work for them. And that is not fair' (TES, 29 August 2008, p. 27). In September 2008, he was complaining again, to the CBI, about employers who 'may not seize the opportunity of the budget' being offered them by government and who are not 'prepared to lead'.

To understand what is happening, one needs to understand that employers are not, on the whole, being offered *training* at all, let alone the training they want. Although these programmes are consistently described in official documentation as 'demand-led', employers cannot actually demand (or request) training that meets their own perceived needs. They are, instead, offered a very different and far more circumscribed opportunity: namely to have a limited subset of their workers accredited with one of a limited set of qualifications. These qualifications are themselves of a very particular type. Governmental control of education and training now goes well beyond the general categories on which money can be spent[14] and dictates what can be funded, taught and accredited at a level of detail never attempted before.

---

13 Responses to questions tabled by David Willetts, MP: HC Deb, 10 February 2009, column 1905W, and HC Deb, 26 November 2007, column 171W.

14 Although disbursements are technically the job of the quangos described, in most recent years the latter have had no authority to move money between categories of expenditure. If one category was overspent, funds could be moved into another only by the department.

Central direction of content and delivery

A system in which providers are paid by a centralised agency, through detailed contracts, to deliver a specified number of specific qualifications, has to have a centralised price list to match: this has duly been created. At its core is a 'qualifications framework' which assigns every qualification to a level – originally one of five levels, but now one of eight. If a qualification is to appear in the framework and be eligible for any form of public support it has to go through a long and increasingly complex process of being approved and accredited by several different quangos.

These make very specific demands about the structure of the qualification – currently, every non-university qualification in the country is being forced to restructure itself around a 'credit framework' created by one of the quangos, the QCDA.[15] Different bodies check a qualification's content; its procedures for assessment; quality control; appeals procedures; its vocational relevance where appropriate (in relation to the country's 'skills needs'); and critically, for the funding authorities, they ascribe to it not just a level but a status as a 'full' or 'partial' award. (The system's quantitative targets are expressed in these terms.) The result determines both how much a provider gets paid and the relative priority attached to contracts that include it: including, for example, whether it is eligible for inclusion in Train to Gain. Box 2 reproduces the first few paragraphs of the guidance explaining what is required if a qualification is to meet 'full Level 2' status: comparable documents exist for other levels.

When journalists are discussing 'Level 2s' and 'Level 3s' they

---

15   The QCDA – Qualifications and Curriculum Development Agency – is one of the successor bodies to the QCA – Qualifications and Curriculum Authority – some of whose functions were recently split off into Ofqual.

tend to explain them in terms of their best-known exemplars. So a Level 2, for example, is 'the same as' a GCSE grade A–C, a Level 3 is 'the equivalent of A-level', and a 'full Level 2' is 'the same as' five GCSE grades A–C. 'Up to a point, Lord Copper ...' is probably the politest response one can muster, when reading this. These equivalences are indeed established, in the sense that they are used in counting progress towards government targets, reporting on the government's attainments, and deciding how much people will get paid for offering a particular course. But only in the looking-glass world of modern English education policy would anyone really claim that a 'full Level 2' in Customer Care, awarded at the workplace on the basis of fifteen hours' contact time, was 'equivalent' to, say, A to C passes in English, Maths, Chemistry, French and History at GCSE.

To anyone outside, this system is completely opaque. (This is one reason why journalists never write about it.) Employers have quite consciously given up trying to understand what is going on. When one examines actual hiring practice one finds that, at sub-degree level, they look at and give credit to only a very few long-standing qualifications, mostly GCSEs and A-levels.[16] The people providing training and education in the post-compulsory sector, meanwhile, must spend large amounts of their time trying to keep up with the latest changes to payment and eligibility schedules, while the bodies that set and award qualifications are forced continually to redesign and reaccredit them in line with new requirements.

One distinctive feature of the current English training sector is the importance of a number of large private sector 'providers',

---

16 See Jenkins and Wolf (2002, 2005). In some occupational areas, they may also pay attention to a small number of long-established vocational awards.

Box 2 Excerpt from 'Qualifications and Credit Framework'

Full Level 2 Guidance for Awarding Organisations (AOs) regarding the interim full Level 2 definition and confirmation process in the Qualifications and Credit Framework (QCF) (Learning and Skills Council).*

1. This guidance has been developed to assist Awarding Organisations to understand the criteria Sector Skills Councils (SSCs)/Standard Setting Bodies (SSBs)/Sector Bodies (SBs) will use when setting full Level 2 threshold for their sector, sub-sectors and occupations, and to identify key considerations that will need to be taken into account when designing new full Level 2 qualifications in the QCF.
2. In November 2008 the Secretary of State agreed an interim definition for full Level 2 until 31 August 2010. The interim full Level 2 definition for QCF qualifications is based on a threshold of 13 credits with SSCs/SSBs/SBs responsible for determining the content for their sectors, sub-sectors and occupations. They also have the flexibility to set the threshold higher or lower than 13 credits in accordance with their sector requirements. LSC has been remitted to disseminate this definition and to support all stakeholders in the identification of full Level 2 and to undertake monitoring and evaluation of the definition in order to inform a final definition for 2010/11 onwards.
3. As part of the implementation of the interim definition, LSC expects that SSCs/SSBs/SBs and AOs will work closely together. Collaborative working will be essential to ensure that vocational qualifications approved as full Level 2 in the QCF meet the needs of employers and learners. We expect

that SSCs/SSBs/SBs will be communicating decisions on sector thresholds with Awarding Organisations to enable them to develop qualifications that can populate the QCF. LSC will continue to work with Awarding Organisations through the Awarding Organisations' Advisory Group and has made a commitment to the Federation of Awarding Bodies (FAB) and to the Joint Council for General Qualifications (JCQ) to ensure early dissemination of SSCs/SSBs/SBs' decisions.

4. As already stated, as part of the wider implementation of the QCF and vocational qualification reform, LSC will be using the Sector Qualification Strategy Action Plans (SQSAPs) to inform funding eligibility decisions, and SSCs will advise LSC on which key vocational qualifications should be funded. In the context of full Level 2, LSC will be reviewing the funding priorities to take account of the new interim definition to ensure public funding is supporting the right provision. Please note that funding rates for qualifications are determined by the input and therefore not all full Level 2 qualifications will be funded at the same rate.

*The original document can be consulted in full on the 'providers' section of the LSC website, which also provides access to the – literally – thousands of documents that have been issued relating to specific programmes, funding changes, audit, assurance etc: www.lsc.gov.uk

who negotiate major contracts with government (generally the LSC) to provide training. Such 'training providers' play a key role in delivering apprenticeships. They are also heavily involved in locating and signing up companies to participate in Train to Gain, which represents the apogee – or nadir – of recent policy trends.

In 2007, the chief executives of the two largest players in this sector gave evidence to the House of Commons Select Committee on Education and Skills on the mechanics of such contracting. As one of them explained, in Train to Gain there are fourteen forms required per learner, while in apprenticeship:

> We have 17 forms to fill in when we take on a learner and that takes over two hours before we have even started and we lose a number of people because they just cannot be bothered to go through the process, even though we hold the pen for them ... To put it into perspective, I have got something like 50 people who are employed full time on processing bits of paper, which is inordinate waste.[17]

It is absolutely necessary to a provider's survival that most 'learners' (*sic*) pass their qualifications, which means that *the less they actually have to learn when they start, the better*. Payment is heavily 'output-related', meaning that providers, whether private or colleges, receive full payment only if the individual gains the qualification. The proportion of funding which is paid only on completion has varied over the years. Output-related funding was first introduced in the late 1980s because of concerns over the high numbers of people who did not complete their courses, and its effect on quality has attracted criticism ever since.[18] The impact obviously varies, however, with the proportion of funds allocated this way.

In general, the level of output-related payment has tended to be higher for private than for public sector provision, but it has increased in recent years, and is very high for Train to Gain. As one experienced LSC official explained to me, 'It is the harshest

---

17   See House of Commons Education and Skills Select Committee 2007: Q273, Q274, supplementary memorandum from Dan Wright.

18   See Stanton (1996) for a full discussion.

and tightest of our methods. Train-to-Gain providers are paid per learner, on a month-to-month basis, and so only once a learner is recruited, and retained. It is monthly, in arrears, with 25 per cent paid only on successful completion.'

There are also very demanding regulations associated with payment claims, involving submission of full and detailed paperwork to validate each individual claim. These reflect policy (and suspicion) at ministerial level: on occasions when quangos such as the LSC have attempted to reduce the level of record-keeping and detailed submissions this has been countermanded at the very top.[19]

The result is that Train to Gain funding just about covers certification and administrative costs, but leaves almost nothing over with which to actually train anybody. The programme's own regulations acknowledge this, in that they demand 'at least' (and so in effect assume no more than) a total of *fifteen hours* of direct contact between the 'learner' and the 'provider', even when the contract is for a 'full Level 2 award' (see Box 2 above). And that is fifteen hours in total, not per week, or per month, or per term. College providers estimate that they need to allow for (and pay for) seven separate trips to a workplace in order to collect the relevant paperwork and carry out the necessary assessments for a typical Level 2 NVQ (National Vocational Qualification).[20] So it is hardly surprising that, as acknowledged by everyone directly involved in delivery, people are simply being certificated for skills they already hold.

Ministers under attack for falling student numbers argue that enrolments are not what matter, but what is being learned – and the important thing is the huge numbers of 'full' qualifications

19   Personal communications.
20   Personal communications.

being obtained. Yet study after study shows that these qualifications mostly do nothing for people's earnings. Low-level
vocational awards, of the type purchased through Train to Gain
contracts, and through much previous, government-encouraged
activity, are associated with low, non-existent or even negative
wage returns (see Chapter 7).[21] Given the circumstances in which
they are obtained, this is hardly surprising: Box 3 recounts the
circumstances under which NVQs were gained in a workplace
hand-picked by the Learning and Skills Council. By now only
ministers and top officials – and perhaps not all of them – can
still believe that this obsession with piling up certification is doing
anything for the nation's skills or productivity.

The different parts of this madhouse are totally intercon-
nected (and, fortunately, unique to this country). Targets lead to
contracts for specified qualifications, and force providers to enrol
students for things they can do already. Detailed contracts require
centralised lists of eligible products and the prices to be paid for
each. That, in turn, creates the 'need' for levels, and categories,
and deciding what each is 'worth', and for rules about what is
required to go into a particular level or category; and, with every
new query, there are yet more detailed additions to the central
rule book. Everything here has its own crazy logic.

The ultimate driver is central government's belief that one can
educate into growth, and that 'vocationally relevant' education
should be prioritised. This belief characterised the Tory adminis-
trations of the 1980s and 1990s as well as the New Labour ones
of the last twelve years. In the latter's case, however, driving up
qualification levels has been not only the centrepiece but almost

---

21   See especially Table 7; also Wolf (2008) for a full discussion of the evidence on
     returns to low-level vocational awards.

Box 3 A Train to Gain success?

In a recent Radio 4 *File on 4* programme, the Learning and Skills Council was asked by the BBC to put them in touch with a 'T2G' success story: they were duly linked up with Crewe Football Club, where thirty stewards had received their NVQs; free to them and at a cost to the taxpayer of £1,200 a head. This was good news for the club because, armed with these certificates, they were legally able to dispense with paying local police £40,000 to cover each match. But new skills? As far as the highly experienced and middle-aged staff were concerned, they had learned nothing: they simply had a certificate to attest, legally, formally and as a contribution to national qualification targets, that they possessed the skills they had been practising for years.

the totality of the government's policy for actively improving British productivity, with large budget increases justified on these grounds. As such, the policy must be judged a comprehensive failure.[22] In this context, the following points are notable:

- There has been no increase in the trend growth of British productivity since 1997. Any reductions in the gap between UK productivity and that of its major competitors have been the result of the latter's worsened performance rather than our improvement.
- Wage returns to most of the qualifications prioritised by government are low or zero at best.

---

22 See, for example, Keep et al. (2006); Abramovsky et al. (2005); Griffith (2007); and Wolf et al. (forthcoming).

- In spite of large authorised increases in spending, and in spite of ever-tighter control of the minutiae of spending and audit, there has also been a complete failure of budgetary control. This is most clearly manifest in the FE colleges' building programme, where the DIUS-controlled Learning and Skills Council has overspent its capital budget by amounts estimated to range upwards from £2.7 billion.[23] It is also evident, however, in the large underestimate of funds required for student maintenance grants, requiring last-minute reallocation of major sums within the overall departmental budget (2008) and in the sudden reduction of institutional grants (to both colleges and school sixth forms) which occurred in early 2009.[24] In early 2009, restrictions on how Train to Gain money is used were also relaxed suddenly, officially as a response to recession and rising unemployment, but also because of officials' panic (and ministers' anger) that funds were not being spent (see above). The LSC was urged by government to disburse funds as fast as possible (with senior executives receiving bonuses on the basis of how much they managed to spend). The sector believes that, as a result, a

---

23 See Foster (2009), which points out that DIUS attends virtually all the relevant meetings and committees as an observer; and House of Commons Innovation, Universities, Science and Skills Committee (2009).

24 Grant letters were sent announcing allocations for 2009/10 which were substantially below what had previously been announced, and had formed the basis for institutions' planning and hiring decisions. Although the letters came from the LSC, they made it clear that the reductions originated with and were approved by DIUS. Emergency funds were found as principals pointed out that they would be unable to accommodate sixteen-to-eighteen-year-olds with a statutory entitlement to education, but grants for 2009/10 are expected by many colleges to fall short of what is required to meet their statutory responsibilities, let alone increased demand at a time of recession.

major overspend will take place here too.[25]

- The supposed beneficiaries of this approach have been manifestly unconvinced of its value. If the 'skills' programmes that the government promotes are indeed as economically relevant as it believes, and superior to previous provision, then companies should be willing to share costs (especially once their early experiences prove positive) and students/ trainees should also be willing to pay a substantial contribution. This has not occurred. Indeed, it is the case that:

  – The proportion of FE college expenditure obtained from fees is tiny (7 per cent) and has remained largely unchanged in recent years (see Fletcher and Perry, 2008). Although there are no comprehensive comparative data, fee income appears to have been much higher as a proportion of college income in the post-war decades.

  – Subsidised (but highly controlled) training programmes which explicitly require a substantial matching contribution from employers have been unable to disburse more than a small proportion of earmarked funds.[26]

  – Workplace programmes that were very highly subsidised, and offered to employers on the assumption that they would lead to large productivity gains, ended once the subsidies ended. A large study of recent programmes of this type – all delivered in line with specific rules on content and delivery – found that employers did not continue the training using their own resources

---

25 Personal communications.

26 This applies most clearly to Train to Gain funding for higher-level qualifications.

once the subsidy ended, and also did not believe the programmes had any impact on productivity (see Wolf et al. forthcoming).

So, are things that bad in the further education sector? Yes, they are. Because institutions take time to develop, it is not usually a good idea to blow things up, and start from scratch. But this sector has tested government's ideas about targets, output-related funding, central planning of curriculum, and multiple quangos to the point where they have destroyed the system. Money goes on administration, not teaching; more and more qualifications are worthless; the underlying incentive structures are deeply dysfunctional. The waste runs into billions. The next chapter therefore goes back to first principles, as a prerequisite for a complete rethinking of how further and adult education should best be organised.

3 SHOULD WE SUBSIDISE POST-COMPULSORY EDUCATION AND TRAINING FOR INDIVIDUALS? THE ECONOMIC CASE

Why might one spend public money on further and adult education? In light of the chaos and waste described above, might it not be better for the state to withdraw entirely from any involvement?

Answering this question requires that one think about the whole of post-compulsory education, because the arguments for and against state involvement in FE colleges or workplace training draw on exactly the same arguments as those for and against state funding of universities. Modern states all make some sort of distinction between school, university and non-university post-compulsory education, but this is actually a very misleading way to think about funding (or educational opportunities). To draw an analogy with medicine, there are major differences between the institutions and the activities that characterise general practice in medicine (still dominated by the self-employed), and hospital-based intensive care. Nonetheless, they are clearly both 'about' individuals' healthcare. Education is the same. There are plenty of differences in prestige, day-to-day priorities and location, but, underlying this, a common field of activity.

As has been observed in many other contexts, the fact that we think people should all be able to afford something does not mean it has to be provided directly. We do not, in wealthy countries, think it acceptable that people should starve or go hungry, but we do not provide food directly to the poor, or sell it to them at special rates in separate shops. Instead, we make sure that there is an adequate level of income redistribution and leave people to get on with spending their income as they wish and decide for themselves exactly how much of their disposable income goes on food, and of what sort.

So should any education be paid for by the state? Or can and should it be left entirely to individuals and to individual institutions, such as charities and employers? If there *is* a case for state involvement, then what institutions and mechanisms are best able to provide subsidies of the right sort to the right places with little waste?

In the case of children under a certain age, there is a well-developed and generally (though not universally) accepted argument that the state should ensure that they are educated and that a certain level of expenditure per child should be guaranteed. This is because of the risk that a child's life will otherwise be blighted by the mischance of being born to a parent who has no interest in its education.

A child has neither the financial resources, nor the information and understanding, to act independently of and contrary to the wishes of its parents or guardian. Compulsory education laws, accompanied by available free schooling, allow the state to act *in loco parentis* and ensure that children are educated whatever their family circumstance. Such laws are the norm in any state that can afford them; although there are large variations in the detail of what is demanded, and supplied.

However rich and however nannyish the state, the moment does arrive when young people are considered old enough to make decisions of their own, and old enough to enter the labour market as regular employees. From then until they die they may, or may not, undertake additional activities that are 'educational' in the broadest sense of the word. These may include a PhD in physics, training as a goldsmith or a fishmonger, a degree in English literature, a class in spoken Italian, guitar lessons, yoga sessions, driving lessons, a bartender's certificate, creative writing classes, a higher diploma in electronics … Are there good reasons for the state to get directly involved in paying for any of this, over and above ensuring a reasonable level of income equalisation?

The reality of government support for post-compulsory education is that it has tended, throughout the world, to grow rather piecemeal, and for a variety of reasons. The theoretical arguments in favour of subsidies, however, are quite limited in number. This chapter and the next three examine them in some detail, starting with the supposed link between education and economic growth which dominates current political discourse. Then we will look at workplace training, and at the special case of apprenticeship. Finally we will consider non-economic reasons for supporting education which previous generations, including their political elites, have considered so much more important than we do. In this chapter, I will argue the following:

- There are some good reasons (as well as some very bad ones) for subsidising *individuals'* purchase of post-compulsory education and training, but none for telling them exactly what they can and cannot purchase. Adult individuals are unquestionably the best judges of what education and training is appropriate for them.
- There are reasonably good arguments for governments

to provide clear information on availability and quality of education and training opportunities.

• There are strong arguments against governments becoming closely involved in the design of courses, not just because they are generally far removed from individual demand and preferences, but also because it directly undermines their ability to provide objective information.

Human capital, growth and market failure: the economic arguments for government funding of post-compulsory education and training

In recent years, UK government policy for all post-compulsory education – especially in England – has been increasingly dominated by economic arguments about the 'need' of the country for more skilled and more qualified workers (the two are taken to be synonymous). These arguments are couched in terms of 'UK plc', and the 'knowledge economy', and invoke the terrors of foreign competition, and especially the hundreds of thousands of graduate engineers supposedly being produced by India and China. They are used by ministers to justify both major investments of taxpayers' money in various forms of post-compulsory education and training and the progressive concentration of government assistance on a limited subset of education and training activities. The 2006 Leitch report, which was commissioned, accepted and is currently being implemented by the government, exemplifies the trend.

Although New Labour has embraced these ideas with enormous enthusiasm (see Kay, 2003), their influence dates back to the 1970s and 1980s. They have been internalised, and are offered uncritically, by large numbers of businessmen and civil servants as well as by politicians. These groups genuinely believe it to be self-evident that we are failing to produce the skills that the economy needs, and will continue to do so without government intervention. It is apparently 'good' for growth for a government (rather than its private citizens) to be spending a high percentage of GNP on education. Yet it is also seen as 'bad' for growth – often by the same people – to be at the top of the international league in terms of tax rates and the overall share of national income spent by government. Why might that be?

Human capital

The argument goes like this. Economic growth is fuelled by education and training – any and all education and training – because they create 'human capital', which makes workers more productive. People recognise this, and are willing to study and train because they can expect higher wages as a result. Left to themselves, however, they train only to 'sub-optimal' levels; while employers also face constraints which lead them to train less than they 'should'. For all these reasons, the state should provide direct, earmarked funding for post-compulsory education and training.

The term human capital must rank as one of the most successful conceptual coinages of the past century. It owes its popularity and influence to the Nobel Prize-winning economist Gary Becker, whose book by that name (1993 [1964]) is concerned with the way in which individuals' skills contribute to economic productivity and growth in parallel to the contributions made by other forms of capital. Capital may be defined as something that is not entirely used up in the production period under examination, but remains a source of future production. 'Human' capital is seen as something embodied in individuals which contributes to production and economic growth. It is created through 'activities that influence *future* monetary and psychic income by increasing the resources in people. These activities are called investments in human capital' (ibid.: 11, emphasis mine).

In a market economy, there is a link between the skills people have – their 'human capital' – and how much they earn. People clearly see this link. Neither teenagers nor adults need convincing of the relationship between getting a degree and earning more; getting a place on a competitive, high-status apprenticeship scheme and acquiring valuable skills; or, indeed, between having a driving licence and being able to apply for large numbers of jobs from which they would otherwise be barred.

In the past, parents paid for their children to be taken on as apprentices. In some of the world's poorest countries, parents pay staggering proportions of their incomes for private schooling because the quality of state schooling is so poor; and do so for explicitly 'vocational' reasons – to help their children get better jobs in the future (see Tooley, 2009). Introducing fees for universities in England (or elsewhere) has had no impact on enrolment levels, and private fee-paying universities are also growing rapidly around the globe, providing degrees to students whose motivation is overwhelmingly vocational.

Some people argue that education should be subsidised because it is good for people's future earnings. But in itself this is a bizarre argument – in that case why not subsidise the opening of a burger bar; a massage parlour; or a hedge fund? (See Box 4.) If someone benefits from something, as a private individual, then why should someone else pay for it? And if the jobs people get

Box 4 Subsidised education and the public good

People often argue, with total conviction, that having their education subsidised serves the public good, and is something for which taxpayers should be happy to pay. This is because they will earn more once they have (typically) their degree, and so will pay higher taxes than if they had not gained the education, and educational credentials.*

To see why this is nonsense, try a little substitution: 'The taxpayer should pay for my university degree because in the future I will earn more as a result and so pay higher taxes' can become 'The taxpayer should pay for me to set up a restaurant because I will then generate profits and pay higher taxes than if I go on working for someone else as a cook'. Or 'The government should pay all the infrastructure costs for this housing development I am considering. That way I will make a large enough profit that, as well as paying my taxes, I can afford to give some of it to local charities'. The arguments are parallel.

If someone is financially better off as a result of their education, then they are indeed better off. They are not paying to the government, in taxes, all that they have gained, or anything like it. So why should other people – fellow taxpayers – pay more tax than at present in order to give the fortunate an ever greater return on their already very safe investment?

*Economic theory is very clear: individuals should pay for things that bring private benefit (such as higher incomes), the taxpayer for social benefits in excess of private benefit. It is sometimes argued that those who work alongside the highly educated also earn more as a result, because everyone becomes more productive in a highly educated workplace, but I know of no good empirical evidence to support this claim.

after completing their education do not pay enough to cover the cost of the education and training (including wages forgone) then one might reasonably assume that the skills are not economically worthwhile anyway.

So is there any reason to suppose that education spending by adults – meaning, in this country, anyone of eighteen or over – might be different, on economic grounds, from other forms of 'investment'? That is, is such spending different enough to justify an undefined but apparently large amount of tax revenue being directed towards it? There are three factors that can and should be taken seriously, and which, though they sound very similar, are in fact quite distinct. They are risk; uncertainty; and ignorance.

Risk, uncertainty and ignorance: the individual's problems

There are three reasons why individuals might undertake less education and training than makes sense for them, in terms of economic returns and job prospects, and where, in theory, government might therefore want to intervene and spend money. All apply in exactly the same way to university- and non-university-based provision. They are:

- risk aversion;
- uncertainty and consequent unavailability of credit;
- ignorance.

Risk, uncertainty and credit

It is often argued that post-compulsory education, including university study, has to be made 'cheap' (free or subsidised) because it is hard for individuals to pay in advance for something whose benefits are long-term. There is some genuine evidence for this, not just as a coherent argument from first principles, but as something that has a major impact on people's choices and behaviour if left unaddressed. There are good reasons to think that many people, especially from poorer backgrounds, are risk averse and that this may make them – in total – undertake less education and training than they 'should', on economic grounds. And there are also good reasons to conclude that the uncertainty of the labour market creates major barriers to obtaining credit for a large part of the population, with the same result.

Suppose that you are thinking of training as a computer programmer. The course, though difficult, can lead to a good, high-paying job – but in cities different from the one you live in. If you know (roughly) the pass level, your own abilities, where the jobs are and how many of them you could take, then you can calculate (again roughly) how likely it is that paying for the course and giving up your current job will pay off. You probably won't do any incredibly complicated arithmetic, but rough calculations of that type are exactly what people do, all the time, when making decisions – including when they take out loans to pay for an MBA and when they take out a mortgage.

Suppose you think it is worth it – the risk is low, the probable return high. Will you be able to find the money?

Banks will lend for an MBA – a well-known, high-volume, high-return degree. For anything less lucrative and less well established, however, it will probably be much harder to obtain private funding. If it is possible at all, it may be only at a very high interest rate, which makes the probability of profiting look much less. Markets may develop some financing mechanisms – grandparents all over Japan start saving for university fees through well-established schemes the minute the baby is born – but the problem of credit availability is real. So, too, is the impact of economic cycles. If you face the possibility of starting repayments, or even simply servicing your loan, at a time when the economy is in recession, this will affect your willingness to borrow even though, medium- or long-term, what you are doing seems like a very good economic bet.

At present, in the UK, the government makes credit easily available – at subsidised rates – for full-time university undergraduates, but not for other students. No good specialised alternatives have emerged for other student/trainee groups; and in general, worldwide, private sector loans for education and training are hard to obtain in countries where there is no governmental involvement or government guarantees.[1]

The difficulty of obtaining credit, as well as people's reluctance to borrow commercially, reflects the fact that, while overall education and training clearly 'pay' at the individual level, there are quite high levels of uncertainty. This affects institutions' willingness to lend and individuals' willingness to borrow.

So uncertainty means that governments may play a very important role as financial intermediaries and guarantors. This point is made by Barr and others in their arguments for governments to provide and underwrite income-contingent loans for university students (see Box 5). These arguments were accepted by the Labour government, which in 2004 introduced both higher fees for students and income-contingent loans to cover them (while also, it should be noted, maintaining high levels of direct subsidy: fees cover only a small part of degree costs).

The barriers to participation created by uncertainty are,

---

1 *Encyclopedia of Higher Education* (1992 and forthcoming): entries on finance, loans and student support.

obviously enough, more serious the poorer the potential student because they are the ones who will be least able to cover costs from their own or their family's resources.[2] The problem is compounded by the fact that poorer families are also generally more risk averse.

Risk is calculable, rather than another word for uncertainty. It also (unless it is zero) indicates that there is a definite possibility that something will not happen, as well as that it will. People's willingness to accept a given level of risk varies considerably, as we know from a wide range of laboratory-based studies, and from analysis of 'real-life' behaviour.[3] Someone who is not very well off, or who has few affluent family members, may very well be 'risk averse' compared with those with larger reserves – either of cash or of contacts and sources of support if things do not turn out well.[4] So willingness to borrow, or undertake a given type of education or training, may differ by individual background. As a result, there is likely to be a differential shortfall in the extent to which individuals undertake the 'human capital formation' which they believe to be potentially worthwhile; and a potentially important role for government in offsetting this.

Overall, the existence of both uncertainty and quite high levels

---

2   A further economic point is worth making here. Why is family support so widespread for the provision of education? One reason is because the borrowers (i.e. potential students) find it difficult to 'signal' to the bank their intent, conscientiousness, etc. How does the bank distinguish a potential hard-working student from the rest? The potential student may be able to signal this by providing collateral for a loan, but this is unlikely to be possible for a young potential student. One way to resolve this problem is for the family, who can judge the intentions of the family member better, to lend the money.

3   See e.g. Siegrist et al. (2005) (and other papers in the same volume).

4   They may also be treated as a worse credit risk and find it objectively harder/ more expensive to get credit.

Box 5 Income-contingent loans

A national system of income-contingent loans for university undergraduates is now central to the organisation and funding of higher education in England, Wales and Northern Ireland and a number of other countries (though not Scotland). Students are required to pay fees that cover (some of) the costs of their degrees, but have automatic access to loans that are guaranteed by government. They repay them only as and when their post-education earnings reach a threshold; and repayment is tapered in line with earnings. In England, these tuition fee loans – along with maintenance loans (towards living expenses) and grants for eligible students – are administered and collected by the Student Loans Company, established and underwritten by the government. The Student Loans Company currently provides loans and grants to a million students annually and is administering loans made to a further 2 million ex-students.

The arguments for income-contingent loans have been elaborated most clearly by Nicholas Barr (Barr, 2004; Barr and Crawford, 2005; Friedman, 1955; Glennester et al., 1968). They address directly the problem that individual borrowers face both risk and uncertainty in deciding whether to borrow for higher education; and that lenders do the same. There is none of the security that exists in the house mortgage market (where, if the borrower defaults, the lender can seize the property); poor borrowers, whose families cannot provide security, will therefore be disproportionately affected.

Loans underwritten by the government, and income-contingent repayments administered by a publicly created body, spread the risk, and allow for efficient lending, and an interest rate that is more or less the same as the (very good) rate at which British governments can borrow. They also make it easy to collect on the loans. Predictions that higher fees plus loans would reduce student numbers and restrict access have proved to be wrong (both in this country and elsewhere). The UK government has chosen to further subsidise the interest rate charged on loans, and to make a very large number of maintenance grants, both of which enormously increase the long-term cost of the system; but neither of these decisions follows from the underlying logic of the approach.

of risk creates barriers both to the availability of credit and to the general willingness of individuals to undertake post-compulsory education and training. Sometimes, of course, they might have been wrong, and this is money well saved. But quite often, they will have been right: and they will suffer economically compared with what might have been, as will the economy overall. So there is a genuine case to be made here for government intervention, either by direct subsidy of provision, which lowers the price people pay and so makes them more willing to undertake a given education option, with given uncertainty and risk, and/or by providing credit under non-market conditions.

All the arguments for such intervention apply in exactly the same way to all forms of post-compulsory education. There is, for example, no obvious reason why student loans should be available for university study but not for apprenticeship. We return to this point when evaluating current UK, and especially English, arrangements in Chapter 7.

Ignorance

Ignorance is the third reason why an individual may fail to under-take economically beneficial, and valued, education and training. It can manifest itself in a variety of ways. Some people may not realise that education 'pays'. More plausibly, many people may not know precisely how well different forms of education and training pay. Most people find it hard to know the quality of specific providers of education and training. And providers of education and training have rather little incentive to provide large amounts of information about the things they do less than brilliantly, and strong incentives to exaggerate the benefits of what they offer. They may also find it very difficult to collect and provide robust information on the relative benefit of their particular courses and offerings, even if they are willing to do so. Overall, consumers of education and training may find themselves having to make choices with very imperfect information and in a situation of 'information asymmetry' (where one party to a trans-action has more or better information relating to it than does the other). Information asymmetry is currently a favourite argument for government intervention, and also a very real problem.

The government may therefore think it justifiable either to improve the availability of information, by providing an unbiased source of data and/or checking on quality, or, more drastically, to change the price that people pay for education (by making it cheaper through subsidies), thus increasing the will-ingness of ignorant learners to enrol and offsetting the effects of ignorance.

It is hard to argue against the idea of providing good objec-tive information. But it is hard not to be deeply sceptical about whether governments can deliver such information or can be trusted to do so.

A major reason for the ever-growing involvement of government in the details of further and adult education provision is its conviction that it needs to meet future economic 'needs' in a way the market will not. But empirical evidence suggests that people in fact tend to be pretty well informed about the job market, at least in their immediate vicinity and for the immediate future. And which of us can claim any more than that, even when we study labour markets or the economy professionally? It is governments which tend to create vast oversupplies of particular skills, by underwriting specialist programmes in areas of supposed 'need'. This does not happen just in this country: the Chinese government created a vast oversupply very recently, for computer programmers whose skills were obsolete long before most had graduated from university. Thus though we may have problems in the market for further education, it does not follow that government action can necessarily improve on the outcome of a more or less free market.

In the UK, if you look at the types of qualification and courses which people have flocked towards voluntarily, as opposed to those the government has tried to cajole or force them into, individuals' decisions look very rational indeed, and the government's quite the opposite. In the 1980s and 1990s, for example, when the return to a degree was averaging around 15 per cent, we saw huge increases in university enrolments. We had an equally wholesale flight from heavily promoted 'youth training' schemes offering National Vocational Qualifications the minute the job market recovered from high youth unemployment. This was also highly rational given the low-to-non-existent returns to NVQs and the negative returns associated with participation in government training schemes for teenagers.[5] Meanwhile, high-quality apprenticeships with big companies such as Rolls-Royce, BT or Honda remained, and are still, hugely oversubscribed (see House of Lords Economic Affairs Committee, 2007).

We know most about the choices made by the young (since they are the most studied). The major barriers to young people taking courses and routes that have high returns are increasingly structural, not the result of ignorance. If the maths and science teaching in your school is very poor, it is pretty irrational to study such subjects in the sixth form – so people don't. If your GCSEs are a disaster, why would you want to stay on at school? None of the courses offered to you will deliver much by way of returns in the labour market, however much the government wants us to believe otherwise. So such people don't stay on. Conversely, when plumbers' fees headed for the sky, queues for places on plumbing courses did the same.

Moreover, there is every reason to suppose that we are becoming more informed, not less. Over 60 per cent of households in the UK have Internet connections, more than 80 per cent of these have broadband, and more than 70 per cent of adults (over sixteen) report regular Internet use. At my own university, students, virtually without exception, report using websites to research their applications, and there seems no reason to suppose that any other university is different; comparable data on search activity for other levels of education are not available to the best of my knowledge.

5   See Wolf (1997). The average return to a low-level NVQ is zero – Dearden et al. (2004), Jenkins et al. (2007) and Wolf (2008).

There are, however, some counter-examples, and some arguments for government involvement in principle. There *are* instances of people not staying in school, not training, not going to university, or not going to as good a university as they might because of their, or their school's, ignorance (see Davies et al., 2009). For example, a very large number of sixth-formers in maintained schools take A-levels that are not valued (and sometimes not even accepted) by the more highly rated universities, whereas almost none in the private sector do so. This seems to reflect genuine ignorance on the part of young people (see Fazackerley and Chant, 2008).

Moreover, researchers have also found a 'principled' reluctance in some state schools to give advice on the relative labour-market value of different qualifications and different institutions on the grounds that it is not for teachers to make 'value judgements'.[6] More generally, as noted earlier, it is not in the interest of colleges, training providers or universities to provide unvarnished information about what people can expect either in terms of conditions when learning (which can be reported quite objectively) or later job prospects (where data are far more speculative and harder to interpret). Consequently, it can be argued, they need to be obliged to do so, especially if they are receiving government subsidy.

So there is something of an information gap and an argument for government to help fill it. But this is hardly a rationale for major government intervention. At the same time there is, unfortunately, good reason to doubt governments' ability to provide objective, unbiased advice under current circumstances.

---

6   Personal communications.

Box 6 Government misinformation (1)

Since the 1980s, UK governments have created a series of new qualifications, and marketed them actively. A good number of these enjoyed a very short life, swept away when they failed to live up to their own hype. (Who now remembers GNVQs, let alone CPVEs?) NVQs and Foundation Degrees, however, have now existed for eighteen and eight years respectively. *National Vocational Qualifications* are highly specific qualifications assessed by observing and recording how people perform on long lists of specific tasks. A billboard campaign around the country informed businesses that workers with NVQs would need no further on-the-job training at all, such was the qualification's thoroughness and currency. When young people proved highly resistant to their charms, a set of full-page advertisements started to appear in broadsheet papers. A typical one in the early 1990s featured a photogenic girl with a computer manual under her arm, and a caption: 'Look out Japan! Lindy's coming'. Lindy was meant to be a trainee on a Youth Training Scheme taking an NVQ. She was actually an A-level student with a sideline as a photographic model.

Foundation Degrees are two-year degrees that are 'targeted upon higher-level skills shortages in growth areas of the economy', and must be developed with employer involvement. Current policy is for most of the growth in higher education to take place through these (with funding earmarked accordingly). Advertising was focused on radio stations; an early example (c. 2003) ran as follows:

Avuncular 'educated' voice: 'Tom, we're delighted. The job's yours.'

Young voice, slightly 'non-received' pronunciation: 'But … I don't understand. You haven't even asked me anything yet.'

Avuncular voice: 'We don't need to. We can see you're doing a Foundation Degree and that's more than enough for us.'

UK governments' activist education policies involve the promotion of certain types of courses and learning over others on the grounds of 'need', and also often extend to the production of new courses and qualifications on a regular basis. This has been especially true in recent years. As Boxes 6 and 7 demonstrate, the corollary of this is government 'information', which, if issued by a commercial producer, would quickly win them a referral to the Advertising Standards Authority.

So, overall, there are good reasons to believe that 'information asymmetries' may be a problem for some learners. But there is much less reason for believing that governments are currently at all well placed to correct them. On the contrary, *if governments are to take on an information-providing role successfully, they need first to denationalise their education systems*. Otherwise, the evidence indicates that citizens will do much better obtaining their information from other sources, and will consistently make more sensible choices for themselves than if they had listened to the advice of government.

Summary

In general:

- There are some good arguments for government expenditure on post-compulsory education and training. Specifically, there is a case for providing financial assistance to individuals, directly or indirectly. If people have to pay full cost, under full market conditions, a combination of risk aversion, uncertainty and credit constraints is likely to lead to 'under-consumption', meaning that people will undertake

Box 7 Government misinformation (2)

Diplomas for fourteen-to-nineteen-year-olds were first offered
to students in autumn 2008, and are designed to combine
vocational content and work experience with academic study,
which makes them a credible university-entrance qualification.
The government had spent £65 million on their development
up to and including 2008, with another £374 million pledged
in the Comprehensive Spending Review. The Diplomas have
a whole website of their own on the government's 'young
persons' website (www.yp.direct.gov.uk). It is made up almost
entirely of videos – proclaiming that 'Taking the time out to
find out about new things doesn't have to mean loads of
reading'. So you can watch a trailer about 'A group of friends
and their Diploma story'; or 'Follow a day in the life of a group
of friends exploring the Diploma'.

The cheery voice on the website tells you that 'You keep
all your options open with the Diploma', that Diplomas
are 'exciting' and offer 'lots of practical experience'. (The
actual requirement is for twenty days' work experience over
two years.) It also claims that 'You'll study things you've
never thought about studying in school and college before'.
('Creative and media' is one Diploma: but Media Studies A-level
already has huge candidate numbers. 'Hair and beauty' is
another Diploma, but hairdressing and beauty qualifications are
among the longest-established, highest-recruiting vocational
routes in both FE and apprenticeship, and quite unsuited to
schools.) The government website also tells people that 'The
Advanced Diploma is the same [*sic*] as getting 3½ A-levels'.
(This is technically true in the sense that it has been awarded
that formal number of points by UCAS. But the implication
that all UCAS points are the same is another case of the false

advertising that governments are unfortunately able to engage in with impunity.)

The Diploma campaign is not, so far, terribly effective, suggesting little enthusiasm for government as a source of unbiased information. Original forecasts were for 50,000 students in the pilot 2008/09 year. In spite of spending almost £4 million on advertising Diplomas in 2007/08 alone,* in November 2008 there were a total of 12,000 pupils enrolled, mostly for the fourteen-to-sixteen Diploma, in a total fourteen-to-nineteen maintained school population of 2,600,000 – i.e. less than half of 1 per cent. In fact, the advertising alone cost £333 per enrolment!

*Written answer by Sarah McCarthy-Fry, MP, to a question tabled by Michael Gove, MP: HC Deb, 8 May 2009, column 435W.

less education and training than would benefit them in wage terms.

- This argument provides a case for a subsidy of – but not total payment for – post-compulsory education and training undertaken for career reasons. Such a subsidy will reduce the prices (and risks) people face at the margin and so increase uptake.

At the same time, three points need reiterating.

First, nothing in this argument implies that individuals will not, on their own, spend money to acquire skills they think will be valuable. On the contrary they will and do, as a look around the world, or a word with any driving school, makes clear. They will, however, probably spend less (though in some individual cases more) than in a world of greater certainty, and probably less, too, than in one of greater income equality because of credit constraints and risk aversion, especially among the less affluent. So this is an argument for subsidies – but *not* for completely free provision.

Second, there is no reason whatsoever to assume that governments will be better able to see the future, and overcome uncertainty, than individuals. They can help by providing *credit and insurance at prices that individuals cannot command in the market*, but not by telling people what the next lucrative occupation will be. At the same time as the English government is engaged in targeting specific, 'high priority' occupations, the Scottish Executive's Review of Funding of Learners expresses clearly the dangers of governments trying to decide exactly how much 'market failure' there is in particular sectors, and fine-tuning support accordingly.

> … one of the key principles underpinning learner support … [is] that it is not appropriate to use differential student support arrangements explicitly to address specific occupational or sectoral labour shortages. There are several reasons for this of which three stand out. First, in the majority of cases, such an approach does not address the principal source of the difficulty: the recruitment or retention of employees … Second, such a policy would add to the complexity surrounding learner/student support arrangements … Third, it is likely to cause the 'bidding up' of student awards by competing occupational interests, leading to a high level of deadweight and the diversion of resources … (Scottish Executive, 2004: 33)

Third, there is no reason, on 'human capital' grounds, to indicate that some adults (age eighteen-plus) should be treated totally differently from others in terms of needing help with access to funding, overcoming risk aversion, or having access to good information. There is no reason why, specifically, we should conclude that full-time students building up human capital in universities should consistently receive more generous assistance than part-time undergraduates, or apprentices, or students in further education colleges, private colleges and training establishments.

We return to all these points in Chapter 7, when evaluating current practice.

4 SHOULD WE SUBSIDISE WORKPLACE TRAINING?

One of the most important characteristics of current UK, and especially English, policy is its emphasis on subsidising work-based training. A very large number of countries subsidise apprenticeships for the young, and these are discussed separately in Chapter 5. Very few, in contrast, provide large sums of money for, or direct benefits in kind to, employers to support training that is directly intended to promote organisations' own specific training needs. Yet, as we saw in Chapter 2, a larger and larger part of England's post-compulsory education and training budget has been directed to this end, most recently through the rapid growth of 'Train to Gain' expenditures.

This is, on the face of it, very odd. The subsidies have, of course, been greeted with enthusiasm by employer associations, notably the CBI. Subsidising existing companies, however, and giving them a further competitive advantage vis-à-vis new entrants, is not usually considered a way to improve economic efficiency and increase social welfare. The policy is, however, based on a theoretical argument which has convinced politicians, civil servants and some leading academics (see e.g. Layard et al., 1994). It derives, once again, from Becker's seminal work, but from a very partial understanding of his arguments. Indeed, I will argue, in this chapter, that *there are no convincing arguments for subsidising companies' regular in-house training, even though that is currently a centrepiece of government policy*.

Training 'on the job'

Many of the activities that increase someone's skills and productivity take place not in a college or university but while they are actually at work. This training process may be quite formal, but often will be very informal; it will involve commitment of other people's time and attention and therefore costs the employer money. Becker argues – absolutely correctly in my view – that such learning is very important for economic productivity, and also in explaining why more experienced workers generally earn more. Of course, this was hardly a new observation: what *was* new was his formal analysis.

This divides on-the-job training conceptually into 'specific' and 'general' components. Specific training is defined as training that is relevant only to a particular company or employer. It makes economic sense for employers to pay for this, in exactly the same way as they pay for new machinery, rent on premises, etc. It is a form of investment, because they can expect to reap the benefit when they sell the resulting output – and at the point when it no longer makes sense in production (and productivity) terms, it will equally make sense for them to stop spending. Even where very specific training is involved, however, it also makes sense for *employees* to contribute to the costs, most obviously by accepting lower wages during training than they would be getting in other jobs. They will receive higher wages once they have acquired the relevant skills, and be in a good long-term bargaining position vis-à-vis their employer, who needs trained workers who possess those particular skills.[1]

---

1   Even though the skills may be valued only in that particular workplace, employers need to feel some confidence that trained workers will not leave for other jobs the minute the training is over. Shared costs promote that confidence, and give employees an incentive to stay post-training, to recoup/enjoy the higher wages.

General training is different. Becker argues that 'general training is useful in many firms besides those providing it; for example, a machinist trained in the army finds his skills of value in steel and aircraft firms and a doctor trained (interned) at one hospital finds his skills useful at other hospitals' (see Becker, 1993 [1964]: 33). Such general skills are actually the more common type – the skills that are valuable to just a single employer are pretty limited. But the more general the skills, the less incentive there is for the employer to pay. If he does, he risks finding that his trained workers will be 'poached' by competitors, who can offer higher wages – in part because they have not paid for the training.

This 'poaching' argument is advanced repeatedly as an argument for government subsidies to employers. Successive UK governments have argued that, in the absence of government action, *market failure* in workplace training will ensue. People who want to acquire skills will not be able to find 'suppliers', even though the training would have major positive outcomes. Employers will hold back from general training, and will instead put time and effort into trying to hire ready-trained workers from elsewhere in the system. Since there are not likely to be many of these (because every other employer is behaving in the same way), the result will be general inefficiency, lower levels of private (and so total social) benefit and a 'low skills' approach to production across the sector (see Finegold and Soskice, 1988; PIU, 2001).

Direct government involvement in funding workplace training is, in the view of successive British governments, the solution. In 2001 a major (pre-election) ministerial speech by David Blunkett on the 'Role of the DfEE in the Economy' stated this standard argument perfectly: 'The government should intervene where the levels and types of training produced by the free market will be sub-optimal,' it argued. 'Left to their own devices firms and individuals *will not* engage in an optimum amount of training' (emphasis mine). Consequently, the minister continued, we have a clear 'economic rationale for government intervention'.[2] In recent years, that intervention has involved making *direct subsidies to firms for in-house training*, which have attracted an ever-larger amount of the education and training budget in both absolute and relative terms.

But in fact, *Becker's analysis did not envisage any such role for government.* On the contrary, his argument was that completely general training, which is useful to all employers, should in principle be paid for *by the employees who receive it*, and *not* by the taxpayer. And of course, if that happens, then the employers will be perfectly happy to supply the training that employees demand.

Poaching and pay scales

Becker believed the employee should pay because it is the person who gains the skills who reaps the benefits, whether they do their learning in the workplace or in a university classroom. Trained employees may take themselves off to higher-paid jobs elsewhere, or stay with the firm that trained them, to whom they are now worth more – something that will be reflected in their pay and conditions. If the employee is 'poached', the employee reaps the benefits; if the employee stays, he or she does likewise.

If the training takes place within a firm, then the obvious way

2   Blunkett (2001: paras 62–4). The key arguments for sub-optimality are presented as (1) the issue of 'general' skills, which we have just discussed; (2) lack of information about skill requirements (also discussed above); and (3) 'spillover' of skills into general growth. While the last of these arguments sounds quite plausible, there is, as noted earlier, actually no concrete evidence for such benefits.

for the employee to 'pay' for it is by accepting lower wages while the training is going on. This argument is what justifies special, low-wage rates for apprentices, and explains the fact that more experienced workers routinely earn more. Indeed, European families in the past often paid for their children's apprenticeships (including, for example, 'professional' apprenticeships with lawyers, architects or doctors) with a direct up-front payment as well as accepting an indentured period of very low or no wages at all: a pattern that still exists in a good number of other countries today.

Why might there be 'market failure', which prevents employees from receiving (and employers from providing) training that will benefit them, and make the economy more productive? Why, in particular, might employees be unwilling to bear the costs of training, via direct payment or, more probably, lower wages during training, with the result that employers under-provide?

One possibility is that people are often not confident of receiving higher wages tomorrow in return for skills today. There are exact parallels to the risk and uncertainty problems for individuals already discussed above. Employees feel unsure that future employers will recognise the skills or offer the higher wage, so accepting lower wages in the meantime can look pretty risky, and they will refuse to do so.

Another possibility is that the employer is convinced – rightly or wrongly – that he cannot make employees bear the costs of the 'general' part of his training. He will therefore have to bear the costs, and duly have the trained worker 'poached' by another employer. The latter will hire the trained individual by offering higher wages than the former can afford because the latter has not paid for the training.

Both sides cannot be right at the same time, for the same enterprise – but their perceptions may routinely reinforce each other and so lead to an undersupply of employer training. British governments are convinced that this does occur, and on a grand scale.

This argument needs to be taken seriously, but it is often presented, as here, as though the underlying theoretical logic leads inexorably to the concrete policy conclusion. In fact, this depends on whether two other conclusions hold. The first is that there really is systematic *and substantial* under-provision of training; substantial enough to worry about and substantial enough to justify the cost of creating and sustaining a major intervention. The second is that direct government subsidies are an appropriate and effective response. The first is unsubstantiated; the second simply untrue.

Regarding the first, there is very little evidence for major and systematic underspending on training by UK employers in relation to the needs of their own enterprises. Some of the relevant literature is general and some specific to the UK. In the past two decades economic research has indicated that in the labour markets of the developed world it is far less difficult for employers to recapture the costs of training than the classic analysis suggests. Also, trained workers do not, in fact, become more likely to quit as a result of 'up-skilling', but, in fact, are less likely to leave.[3] This, in turn, is partly related to the fact that gains from training, in the form of higher wages, are realised to a far greater degree by employees who stay than by those who quit. These findings

---

3   See e.g. Acemoglu and Pischke (1999); Black et al. (2003); Asplund (2004). In general, employer-provided training provides higher returns to those who stay than to those who move employers: no doubt in part because your current employer has a far better grasp of your abilities than any potential one possibly can.

suggest that the specific and the general elements of training may be separate conceptually, but are in practice highly intertwined.

While there is little, if any, evidence that 'poaching' is an issue, governments everywhere have made it very difficult for individuals explicitly to accept lower wages in return for training even if they are willing to do so. Under current institutional arrangements, a UK employee could be willing to share the costs of training with an employer, or, indeed, to pay the entire cost, and still find it difficult in practice to do so. Most individuals are in no position to agree to lower wages than their workmates in return for additional training time. British workplaces are subject to a great many restrictions, relating to equal pay rules, minimum wages, working hours, grounds for dismissal, etc. This is not an environment in which employers or workers will find it easy or appealing to negotiate anything in the way of individualised 'training contracts' with any sort of financial implication.

Although there is no evidence that this has led to systematic, economy-wide under-provision of training, it clearly has led to a number of substantial inequities and distortions.[4] *One result is the rise of the deeply inequitable unpaid 'internship', open in practice only to those with families rich enough to support them.* In some of the most desired occupations (especially but by no means only the media) and in a growing number of developed countries, such internships are both increasingly common and increasingly important as a route into permanent employment (see e.g. Sutton Trust, 2009).

---

4   There are a few specific occupations (notably in construction) where we have clearly been failing to provide adequate training to meet future UK demand for skilled labour. International comparisons make it clear that this is not something inherent to the industries concerned and instead reflects the policy environment established by successive British governments.

Overall, the argument that there is substantial under-provision of training is not well supported by empirical evidence. What of the argument that direct government intervention in workplace training is an appropriate response to the 'market failure' argument? Here, the evidence is that most government intervention has been misdiagnosed, expensive, ineffectual at best, and very probably counterproductive. Again, some of the evidence is general and some UK-specific.

Generally, governments' attempts to increase training volumes through direct action have consistently disappointed. There is no empirical evidence indicating a link between government activities designed to increase employers' in-house training expenditures and changes in productivity or growth rates. This is true whether the governmental activities concerned involve requiring businesses to spend money; providing training directly through government-run schemes; or subsidising enterprises' own training activities.

Historically, the most common government response to supposed market failure has been compulsory training levies on firms: that is, requiring all businesses to spend a minimum amount on training and/or contribute to a centralised training fund. The argument is that everyone will underspend, for the reasons outlined above; therefore a tax is needed which, by falling equally on everybody, will stop there being a 'free-rider' problem.

Training levies are by no means universal: they are, for example, unknown in the USA. They have been embraced by a number of major developed countries, however, notably France. This approach places the burden of paying for the supposed short-fall in training expenditure on employers (with the government somehow estimating – or rather guessing – what level of under-spending exists.)

The UK experimented with training levies in the 1960s and 1970s, channelling levies through Industrial Training Boards which provided training in their industries. The policy was commonly felt to be a failure (and not only by employers), generating highly bureaucratic structures and little effective training. The boards were largely abandoned in the 1980s. An exception was made for the construction industry, which to this day retains the Construction Industry Training Board[5] and a training levy. The industry also has recurrent and acute skill shortages and a very poor record of providing employer-based apprenticeships. More generally, international experience suggests that levies fall disproportionately on small and medium enterprises which pay but receive little benefit (see Wolf, 2002). Large companies are typically able to offset them against large-scale, observable and audit-worthy in-house activity, thus winning exemption from direct payment.

Periods of high unemployment evoke, worldwide, expenditures on special training programmes in which governments try to guess what skills employers will want, or have supposedly been under-providing, and train the unemployed in these. The research literature on public training programmes for the low-skilled, unemployed and redundant is now international and ample, and the results clear. Such programmes have a consistent record of failure, doing nothing for participants' future employment prospects and earnings.[6] If there was substantial under-provision of

---

5   Currently known as 'CITB-ConstructionSkills' (*sic*) in England.

6   See e.g. Heckman et al. (1999). The only exception to the general findings is for large, intensive programmes (of around two years' full-time duration). See Lechner et al. (2004); Richardson and van den Berg (2006).

skills by the market, then it is hard to see why these programmes should be so ineffective in promoting employment and future wages.

As already discussed, in recent years the UK has responded to perceived market failure with a policy of direct subsidies to companies. This is an extremely unusual response. It inevitably favours existing companies over new and potential entrants. It is almost bound to contribute to 'specific' training as well as 'general', because, as we saw above, the two are, in practice, highly intertwined: hence the fact that returns to training are acquired largely by those who do not change employers. The subsidies also favour larger companies over smaller ones, because it is much more profitable for subsidised training providers to work with large companies that can offer large numbers of learners on a single site than with large numbers of small and scattered enterprises. Some companies have become 'providers' themselves, contracted to government to deliver subsidised training to their workers, although the attendant bureaucracy means that most prefer to obtain training from others (see Wolf et al. forthcoming).

Not only is the current UK approach difficult to justify on principle; it is also failing to yield discernible benefits in practice. As already noted, the last seven to ten years, in which funds have been increasingly targeted on workplace learning, have failed to produce any increase in the rate of productivity growth. An evaluation of the 'Employer Training Pilot' (ETP) scheme that preceded 'Train to Gain' (and which provided wage subsidies as well as free training) found that the programme had no significant effect on the total volume of training in the economy, suggesting that employers whose staff were on ETP schemes simply postponed or cancelled previously planned training (Abramovsky et al., 2005). Wage returns to the qualifications that are generally provided range from very low to zero (see Chapter 7). And, as discussed in Chapter 2, employers have shown little inclination to top up government spending, as they might be expected to do if it was providing valuable and productive inputs. In other words, current policies of subsidising in-house training are economically unjustifiable, because they distort choices and benefits. They are also almost entirely deadweight expenditure. They combine an obsession with meeting employers' demands, to the exclusion of individual adults' preferences, with a rigid and prescriptive policy which tells employers what they should want rather than offering them what they do want.

Summary

We return to the specifics of current UK policy in Chapter 6. More generally, and in summary:

- Taxpayers should not be involved in subsidising employers by paying for workplace activity that includes large amounts of firm-specific training
- Individual employees, like all adult citizens, face the problems of risk and uncertainty and access to capital discussed earlier. In many cases, the workplace may be the appropriate venue for acquiring the skills in which they are interested, and this should be allowed. Subsidies should nonetheless be channelled through the individual, and reach employers only via individuals' decisions and commitments.
- Governments need, in this context, to address labour market regulations so as to allow a wider variety of agreements

between employers and employees who wish to acquire skills in the workplace and on the job. They are a probable important source of 'market failures' in the provision of workplace training for adults; and addressing these, not direct subsidy of existing, large employers, is government's appropriate task.

5 EMPLOYERS AS EDUCATORS: THE SPECIAL CASE OF APPRENTICESHIP

In many countries, governments have no direct involvement whatsoever with on-the-job training of employed, adult workers. There is nothing like Train to Gain; no huge apparatus of government-funded bodies setting 'occupational standards' for their sector; no targets specifying how many employed adults should obtain formal qualifications at 'Level 2' (or 3, or 4). If employers want to train their workforce they do so, and pay for it.

Apprenticeships, however, are an important part of the post-compulsory education landscape in almost every country in the world, and one with which many governments do involve themselves directly. They are particularly important in Germany and Switzerland, and therefore attract a great deal of attention as possible generators of economic growth.[1]

In the English-speaking world, apprenticeships are currently viewed somewhat uncritically as highly desirable. Supporting and expanding apprenticeships is one of those policies which every politician endorses without even thinking about it, although this was not always the case. In the late 1970s and early 1980s, reformers saw apprenticeships as restrictive practices, with access controlled by insiders. As such they were criticised both as a way

1   German apprenticeship is famous and the subject of a huge literature; but it is worth noting that there is no comparable regulation, government involvement in or subsidy for adult training.

of denying opportunity and access and as a way of raising wages – in exactly the same way as professions have been and continue to be criticised.[2] Unions, meanwhile, are often highly suspicious of apprenticeships, which they view as a way of securing lower-paid labour under the pretext that these are people 'in training' (see e.g. Ryan, 2004).

Discussions of apprenticeship are often confused by the fact that apprentices may and often do contribute directly to output, especially later in their training. In Germany, there is a considerable body of evidence indicating that, towards the end of an apprenticeship, most employers profit from the apprentice's presence, although earlier on the employer is a net contributor. Moreover, employers may use apprenticeship as a way of recruiting, screening and appointing staff (Johansen, 2000). Some employers with long-standing apprenticeship programmes talk about their 'need' to recruit apprentices, independently of whatever government does (House of Lords Economic Affairs Committee, 2007); and policymakers worry that employers will recruit fewer than they 'should' because of our old friends market failure and fear of poaching.

All this obscures the key fact for any discussion of post-compulsory funding. Apprenticeship involves, and has always involved, in varying degrees, employers offering training *not as*

2 This view was held by many in the Manpower Services Commission (MSC), the quango that spearheaded the Thatcher governments' labour market programmes. Similarly, a key tenet of the MSC's offspring, the National Council on Vocational Qualifications (which created and established NVQs), was that any form of 'time serving' must be outlawed, and that there must be open access to all to demonstrate competence in any occupational area, and be accredited for it. See, for example, the New Training Initiative consultation document (MSC, 1981) and Jessup (1991).

part of the productive system, but as part of the education sector, and being recompensed for this. Apprenticeships developed, independently and all over the world, as a way of training young people for highly skilled jobs, including those of carpenters, printers, artists, scribes, bankers, goldsmiths and tailors. This training took place almost entirely in the workplace because this was the most efficient and cheapest place for it to happen in a world of small businesses and a tiny state. It was typically controlled by the organised guilds, so loathed by Adam Smith and depicted by Wagner in *The Mastersingers of Nuremberg*. These guilds typically had a strong interest in maintaining quality, but also a very strong interest in controlling entry and restricting competition and a resistance to innovation.

In the past, parents paid the employer a fee to take their child on as an apprentice. In this country, it was common for the state (in the form of the parish) to pay employers to take on pauper children as apprentices. With no one to look after their interests, such children were often neglected and used as cheap labour rather than receiving much instruction and care,[3] but the underlying principle was the same.

As formal educational establishments grew, some jobs that in the past had been learned predominantly through apprenticeship ('articles') moved to being largely and sometimes compulsorily university-based. Obvious examples in the UK are accountancy, chartered surveying, pharmacy and the law.

Social scientists have charted the efforts of different occupational groups to become 'graduate professions' as a route to status and higher pay (often through licensing) (see e.g. Wilensky,

---

3   See, for example, Dickens's description in *Oliver Twist*.

1964; Collins, 1990). What has received much less attention is the symbiotic relationship between the occupational desire for prestige and status, government beliefs in the economic benefits of higher education, citizens' demand for an expansion of higher education because it is the route to occupational success, *and the desire of both employers and individuals to have someone else pay for their training.* All these factors have come together in many countries over the last half-century and have fuelled a still-continuing increase in the proportions of young people attending higher education, and in the proportions aspiring to do so (see especially Wolf, 2002; and Brown and Hesketh, 2004).

Meanwhile, other occupations have retained an apprenticeship base, partly because of status issues but partly because formal classroom-based education was manifestly inadequate as a basis for imparting practical and manual skills. They include construction trades, catering, some types of engineering, but also, albeit at postgraduate level, medicine and surgery. Here too, today, it is generally the state which pays, at least in part: for example, in Germany apprentices spend most of their time in the workplace, but a sizeable amount in formal training establishments, and the latter are financed by the state (see Box 8). The other major change, compared with previous years, is that apprentices have become older on average. Many now complete secondary education before starting an apprenticeship, and in countries where this is permitted, increasing numbers are in their twenties or even older.

Apprenticeships are, by definition, designed to produce skilled workers in a particular occupational area. And for that very reason, apprenticeship systems must have surplus capacity and produce more graduates than the economy 'needs' (demands) at the time. This is obvious when one stops to think about it: some people will decide they have made the wrong choice, will get sick, emigrate or drop out of the labour market. And even among those who do not, there needs to be some slack while people change jobs, while employers expand or contract or move.

So apprenticeships are essentially educational institutions and apprentices are essentially students: though they are not *just* students, which makes apprenticeship conceptually confusing and hard to develop or reform. And it is this educational function of apprenticeship which should dominate any discussion of government involvement, either as funder or as regulator. This makes apprenticeship fundamentally different from the training of employed, adult workers to be more productive in their current jobs (Chapter 3), because it is expected and necessary that many apprentices will move on to other employers and, indeed, to different occupations.

The state and the individual: further education and higher education

But does this educational function affect how apprenticeship should be funded? Shouldn't apprentices in fact be paying for their general training, just as employed workers should be? In the apprentices' case, should not the modal approach be a combination of up-front fees (as in the past) and lower wages, rather than, as with adults, lower wages alone?

The answer, I suggest, is that the state does need to be involved for two reasons, both of which underline the common ground shared by all forms of post-compulsory education and training. The first is the exact parallel to the argument set out in Chapter 2.

If we want people to be able to undertake training that they judge valuable, and for which they are in principle willing to pay, then we should also ensure that they do not face barriers because of an absence of credit and of (affordable) insurance against the training not paying off. The absence of credit may arise not because the individual does not have good prospects but because he or she may well find it difficult to signal to potential lenders that there is a good chance that the loan will be paid off (unless the family has collateral against which they can borrow). In the past, whether or not young people could become apprenticed to a skilled trade, or articled for a profession, depended on their family wealth; that is not, and rightly not in my view, something that should happen today.

From an individual's point of view, the same issues of risk and uncertainty arise as were discussed in Chapter 2. There seems no reason why apprenticeship-based learning should differ systematically, in these respects, from learning based in universities or colleges. The reader is therefore referred to the arguments surrounding that problem. The implication is that apprenticeship should be treated exactly like higher education in terms of access to grants and income-contingent or other loans.[4]

The second reason for government involvement is more historically specific (though common to many countries). Enormous subsidies are provided for full-time upper secondary and higher education. It is very common for there to be far less support for part-time study or apprenticeship. But this situation is both highly inequitable and also economically inefficient, in that it distorts individual choices, and it needs to be remedied.

4   Equally, if the apprentice is under eighteen, then they should enjoy the same access to funding as other under-eighteen-year-olds.

Higher education subsidies mean that employers are often able to displace a sizeable part of the training they used to do on to higher education institutions. Even if the training is less specific to their needs, and even without the work the apprentice does, they are often at least as well off as under apprenticeship, if not better off. If governments make it very easy for universities to develop vocationally related degrees, and for the taxpayer therefore to pay for vocational training through the higher education route, individual employers will inevitably recruit as far as possible from graduates. Individuals will also tend to opt for the graduate pathway because it has more general value in the marketplace should they wish to change careers. If, on top of this, governments do not offer apprentices comparable subsidies to those offered to university students, qualified young people will need to be very certain indeed about their career choices to opt for apprenticeships.

As noted above, Becker argued that if someone wants to learn valuable general skills at work, they should be willing to accept lower wages in return for future gain; and apprentices, historically, entered into exactly such a bargain. In return, they obtained skills which it was assumed most of them would take elsewhere. Completing a full craft apprenticeship continues to yield financial dividends in this country (McIntosh, 2004) and not only for those who remain in the trade for which they trained. But the individual returns are much lower than for degrees, in part because the level of subsidy is lower than for full-time college students, as is access to loans and grants. There is no theoretical justification for this difference.

Box 8 Apprenticeships in Germany

Modern German apprenticeships illustrate the essentially educational aspect of any apprenticeship system. Some apprentices stay with their original employer, but the majority move on and many never use the most specific parts of their training at all, any more than large numbers of graduates in engineering, literature or law become engineers, literature teachers or lawyers. It remains financially worthwhile to have completed a German apprenticeship, however, whatever one's later occupation. In both Germany and Switzerland, pressure to expand higher education and to turn large quantities of apprenticeship-based training into classroom and higher-education-based courses has been contained by the structure of the school system, which channels large numbers of young people into courses from which they cannot enter university.

Governments and employers

Suppose we direct subsidies to individuals who wish to undertake apprenticeships for the reasons rehearsed above. Can we not expect a modern version of articles and indentures to be generated naturally? Just as people might pay a university or a provider of IT or language or accountancy training, they can surely also sign up as apprentices – at any age – paying a fee to an employer. And if they win an apprenticeship place they would be eligible for whatever sort of bursary or income-contingent loan for fees and living expenses is available to students on other long-term courses such as degrees. Is there any reason, in that context, for other forms of government activity or involvement with employers? Do we, in principle, need to offer any state subsidy to the *employers* involved in training apprentices as opposed to the apprentices themselves?

First of all, the state does have a role to play with respect to reforming employment law – effectively liberalising it, at least for people in apprenticeships. Recognising and treating apprentices as essentially 'students' – as they were in pre-modern times and still are in countries with large and successful apprenticeship systems – is essential, because it takes them outside normal wage-bargaining procedures. Back in the 1980s, when UK apprentice numbers plummeted, the level of apprentice wages attracted a lot of attention. If these have been negotiated at very high levels, apprenticeship becomes a far less attractive proposition, in terms of the enterprise's own immediate skills requirements, let alone as an educational supplier. And an employer who does take on apprentices then has a very strong incentive to maximise their 'work' contribution and minimise training input.

The negative effects of treating apprentices as workers is currently very evident in the NHS. In the UK – unlike in many other countries – junior doctors in hospitals are in reality apprentices but have the legal (and wage) status of full-time employees ('service providers'). This has always created a tension, since the hospitals and senior staff rely on juniors to provide front-line service to patients while also having an obligation (legal and professional) to ensure that they receive training. In recent years, the tensions have been increased by a combination of the EU Working Time Directive, which reduces enormously the amount of time young doctors can work (and, therefore, gain experience in an apprenticeship mode as well as providing stand-alone service); big pay increases to junior staff which put pressure on employers to keep staff numbers down and extract maximum service output from their juniors; and centrally imposed targets which create major time pressures for delivery of service and make it difficult and risky to allow inexperienced juniors to carry out procedures slowly under supervision. The result is a growing crisis in medical training[5] which derives, very clearly, from the failure to implement a coherent apprenticeship system, albeit compounded by regulation at both the national and EU level.

Second, some form of regulation may be required because of information asymmetry issues. How far these require government involvement and how far employers can be trusted to self-regulate or develop appropriate intermediary institutions depend on institutional factors. In Germany, the employer-controlled Chambers of Commerce have far more power, and greater incentives to control quality, than in the case of, for example, France or the UK. Companies that take on apprentices nonetheless are obliged have staff who are 'Meisters' and fully qualified to supervise and instruct them. Individuals may have a reasonably informed view of the labour market in general, but they are rarely in a position to check the content and quality of individual apprenticeships before they sign up. Moreover, if apprentices are students as far as terms and conditions of employment are concerned, employers have a strong incentive to continue formal apprenticeships well past the point at which the apprentice stops learning new skills (though still bound by indentures).[6] Some

---

5 See, for example, the comments of the president of the Royal College of Surgeons of England: http://www.rcseng.ac.uk/news/surgeons-the-european-working-time-directive-and-august-1st-2009

6 The period at the end of apprenticeship, when the apprentice is productive, is of course one way in which the employer is 'paid' for the training provided. But there are obvious information problems for apprentices when they start their training. In the 1930s it was quite common for employers, especially in hard-hit

organisation needs to provide a credible guarantee of and check on quality.

Finally, some direct payments may be necessary to encourage and enable employers to operate as high-quality educational establishments over and above meeting their own training needs. For most companies, apprenticeship numbers will be small, and recruitment patterns uneven, and without some up-front payments, few will want to undertake the costs of establishing and maintaining a good-quality programme. But we also need to recognise that any grants to employers for apprenticeships are paid because the employers are carrying out an educational function and operating primarily as educational suppliers.

It also needs stressing that, while payments are justified by the educational aspects of apprenticeship, apprenticeship itself is valuable because and insofar as it involves 'real-life' environ-ments which cannot be duplicated in educational establishments. That, in turn, means that a successful apprenticeship programme must recognise and value the reality of a workplace. Successful apprenticeships, whether in Germany or in the smaller-scale, revi-talised approaches of some other European countries (see Box 9), do not demand total uniformity from the workplace in terms of skills covered and equipment used; do not demand large amounts of formal assessment and record-keeping from employers; and do not expect employers to operate as though they were educa-tors first and running a business only second. The opposite is true of our current over-specified, restrictive and bureaucratic apprenticeship 'pathways'. It is this over-regulation, driven by

---

industries, to take on large numbers of apprentices whose substantive training finished long before the end of the indenture period; and who were fired as soon as the indentures ended.

Box 9 Apprenticeships elsewhere

The UK has been obsessed with German vocational education for a century and a half now. Ever since Britain lost its industrial supremacy in the late nineteenth century and became aware of the thorough education offered to young Germans, one government report after another has bemoaned the UK's failure to develop a comparable system of technical schooling or, more recently, of apprenticeship. The economies of the two countries are now more different than they have ever been, with Germany maintaining a far larger manufacturing sector (proportionately and absolutely) than any other European country, and, correspondingly, a demand for large numbers of highly skilled workers for whom prolonged apprenticeship training is the best preparation. Germany is increasingly unusual in the scale and importance and prestige of its apprenticeship system. Even Austria, its German-speaking neighbour with an apparently similar education and training system, has seen apprenticeships decline precipitously in prestige as more and more parents (and students) aim for a university education. Countries such as the Netherlands, France and Ireland, which have revived apprenticeship as a desirable option with genuine labour-market links, have done so on a considerably more limited basis than Germany. What all share is that the workplace part of an apprenticeship is genuinely under employer control.

the publicly funded network of Sector Skill Councils, and not just the fundamental problems in how apprenticeships are financed, which has created the current UK situation, in which record numbers of so-called 'apprentices' co-exist with an apprenticeship system that is failing to produce highly skilled young people.[7]

The importance of workplace experience

As discussed in Chapters 2 and 7, the non-university parts of post-compulsory education and training are, in the UK, and especially in England, subject to levels of central planning and micro-management that are historically unprecedented and internationally extraordinary. This applies to apprenticeship as much as to any other part of the system. Much of the heavy criticism to which current apprenticeship programmes are subject[8] would be addressed immediately if participation and purchasing decisions were genuinely in the hands of would-be apprentices.

It is, however, worth noting that young people can learn two major sorts of skill in a workplace which they cannot learn, or can learn only less effectively, in an educational establishment. The first is the type of skill associated with traditional apprenticeships: manufacturing machine tools, carrying out audits, cutting hair, or operating for cataracts. These are skills that require long periods of training, supervision by up-to-date practitioners and training environments characterised by specialist and often expensive materials and equipment.

The second are general workplace skills of the sort that employers constantly tell surveys that they want, such as

---

7 Growth has been in lower-level (Level 2) qualifications, while Level 3 numbers – required for craft-level skills – have fallen. See the written answer from Sion Simon, MP, HC Deb 2009, column 476W, and House of Lords Economic Affairs Committee (2007).

8 See, for example, Fuller and Unwin (2008); Ryan et al. (2007); Lewis and Ryan (2009); Lewis and Ryan (2009b); House of Lords Economic Affairs Committee (2007).

punctuality and teamwork. You learn the second sort by doing a job; and the research evidence confirms that having held a job has clear positive effects both on your future employment prospects and your future income. But there is no reason to suppose that there is any general 'under-provision' of training in these skills.

There is only a limited subset of occupations in which extensive, complex on-the-job training is required. It is economically illiterate to assume that every employer and every employee will benefit from having large amounts of training attached to every job – some may, many will not. It is a 'sub-optimal' use of funds to try to force apprenticeships on every sector if there is no natural demand for them, or to force every young person who does not want to continue in full-time classroom study to undertake 'practical' training instead. People who do not wish to train should not be forced to do so by government (whether they are 17 or 47).

Equally, if what one is trying to promote is the type of 'employability' that is gained through work experience, then the appropriate policy tool involves job promotion (possibly through job subsidies), not some artificial 'apprenticeship'. UK policy promotes the creation of 'apprenticeships' in each and every sector; and also promotes the idea that they should be of equal length, make equal 'demands' and lead to 'equivalent' qualifications. In other words it involves pretending, wastefully, that many occupations require long periods of specialised workplace training when they do not. 'Retail' apprenticeships – which in this country are entirely a government creation – are an example. The idea that most retail jobs require large amounts of workplace training in specific retail skills before they can be carried out is something to which employers' hiring practices give an immediate lie. Ask yourself who gets Saturday jobs: retail apprentices with a few low

GCSE passes, or nicely spoken A-level students?

If people want to obtain apprenticeships and they are able to do so, that is fine. If not it should be up to individuals when in their lives, where and for what they draw down on any subsidies and loans that are made available for further education.

Summary

Apprenticeships should be thought of as part of the general education system, not as part of on-the-job training, and should be paid for in the same way and on the same terms as other forms of post-compulsory education. This may involve payment by employees to employers in terms of salary sacrifice or direct payment. Alternatively, if payment or loans for other forms of further education are available then they should be made available to employees involved in apprenticeships on the same basis. Apprenticeships are likely to develop freely within labour markets in specific occupations where intensive employer involvement and supervision are involved in training. Employers who offer such training or apprenticeships may well require payments over and above the fees they receive from the apprentices. Practical training courses (including those with work placements) which are not employer-led and employer-based should also be treated in exactly the same way as other post-compulsory courses based in colleges, schools, etc., rather than treated and funded separately, but should not be called 'apprenticeships'. It is also important that employment law does not restrict the forms of employment contract that employers may wish to make with their employees – doing so may well hinder the conditions that will ensure that an apprenticeship benefits both employee and employer.

6 PSYCHIC INCOME AND THE 'GOOD SOCIETY': THE NON-ECONOMIC CASE FOR SUBSIDY

One of the most curious aspects of our increasingly wealthy society is its downplaying of any educational objective for further education. Making us even richer seems always to be the prime concern. This is a contemporary phenomenon, and the English are particularly strongly affected.[1] For several decades, and to an ever greater degree, governments have been focused on the presumed contributions of education and training to raising economic output, especially at post-compulsory level.

Most of the education White Papers and proposals that flow from Whitehall pay cursory homage to the idea that education is about more than developing skills for the workforce, but ministers' and policymakers' hearts are not really engaged. Their speeches are all about the economy, and certainly not about developing 'the wisdom of the entire community'.[2] The Foster review of further education (FE), for example, stated unequivocally that the primary purpose of an FE college is 'to improve employability

---

1   This is highly evident in sixteen-to-eighteen-year-old provision as well, where governments have for decades been designing and redesigning qualifications for less academically successful young full-timers. These qualifications have in common their relentless focus on vocational contexts and subject matter. Contrast this with, for example, the proportion of time that a comparable French, US or Canadian student spends on genuinely 'general' subject matter.

2   The phrase is from Robert Hutchins. Hutchins was chancellor of the University of Chicago and a highly influential writer on education in the immediate post-war period, when he championed the idea of a liberal education. Hutchins (1953: 14).

and skills in its local area contributing to economic growth and social inclusion' (Foster, 2005: 3), which is an accurate reflection of modern policy, but excludes much of the sector's early history and objectives. And post-compulsory, non-university provision in England is currently organised more or less entirely around delivering the targets of the Leitch report, which is occupied entirely with developing 'world-class skills' (*sic*) in order to improve economic competitiveness.

Yet the idea that the only purpose of being educated is to get richer, and that, having got richer, we should then expand education simply in order to get richer still, is both modern and very odd.

It is also especially prevalent in the non-university parts of the post-compulsory education system. These include apprenticeship, workplace training and overtly vocational courses, which are by their nature 'about' workforce skills and development; but post-compulsory, non-university education can also include a very wide range of provision which is not simply about the immediate application of new skills in an occupational context. In the UK, such provision has been progressively devalued, and government policy is to restrict subsidies to courses that are directly and solely intended to promote 'skills' and so-called economic competitiveness.

This is not true of university provision. While the 'pure' skills focus of the non-university sector is generally accepted (or, at least, not much remarked on by the general public and media), whenever a government minister implies that university study should be purely vocational, and directed to immediate job requirements, this attracts headlines and widespread criticism (and fairly rapid retractions).[3] So it is apparently legitimate and

---

3   See, for example, the responses to a speech made by Charles Clarke, when Education Secretary, in which he was reported as having criticised the idea that the

desirable for university students to continue studying music, history or literature; still possible to mount a defence of a liberal, or liberal arts, education at university level; important to have universities that include scholarship, the humanities, philosophy and pure science; but it is not apparently part of an (English) government's concern whether comparable provision exists at post-compulsory sub-degree or non-university level.

This narrowly 'economic' view of education is not in itself the fault of economists or of the economics-based conceptual structure that is largely used to discuss education policy. There is nothing in economics which says that people are only interested in money, and that earnings are the only source of private or social benefit. Gary Becker, the high priest of human capital theory, is quite clear that education and training are not just about financial returns and future wages. Investments in human capital, he writes, involve activities that influence 'future monetary *and psychic* income by increasing the resources in people' (Becker, 1993 [1964]: 11).

In other words, the rewards of education go well beyond economic productivity for society or higher wages for the individuals concerned. But the fact that something is rewarding does not mean the government should pay for it. Is there any justification for government subsidies to post-compulsory education activities – at university or in other parts of the post-compulsory system – which are not intended to increase individuals' productivity as well as their wages? Or do the arguments for subsidies to individuals advanced in previous chapters apply only to vocationally specific provision? And is there any reason why subsidies should

study of medieval history should receive state support; Vasager and Smithers (2003).

be offered to this end only for some students – within the university part of post-compulsory education, and not other parts?

The purposes of education

Our ancestors would have taken it to be self-evident that education was about much more than the economy (though it was always about that too). In medieval times, religious instruction and the saving of people's souls were a central purpose of educational spending; indeed, they still are in many countries. Later, the ideals of developing rational inquiry and logical thought, and the idea that all human beings should have the opportunity to develop and enlarge their minds, became increasingly important. US undergraduate education, with its four-year degrees and delayed specialisation, is the result of an explicit belief in the importance of a broad and liberal education, both for the 'psychic income' (or mental wellbeing) of the individuals concerned and for their behaviour as citizens and voters. The French take it for granted that any course of study, vocational or academic, should contain a strong element of general education, not because it makes people more economically productive – though, ironically, it almost certainly does that too – but because a society *should* be educated, and so should all its citizens. British apprentices follow an increasingly narrow 'skills-based' curriculum;[4] but their German counterparts do not.

The UK has not always been so fixated on narrowly

---

4   The apprenticeship curriculum has effectively been nationalised since the 1980s. A short-lived commitment to broader 'technical certificates' was derailed, largely by the government-financed Sector Skill Councils (House of Lords Economic Affairs Committee, 2007).

utilitarian motivations. The Victorians – in far poorer times – funded museums, underwrote free lectures and promoted education for both men and women. They did so because they thought knowledge and education made people better and more fully human, not just better off. Andrew Carnegie did not fund libraries throughout the UK just so that aspiring careerists could further their ambitions and tradesmen improve their vocational skills.

The fury that drives Hardy in his novel *Jude the Obscure* is over the way Jude is denied the chance to use his mind, not a failure to get a good craft training or a better-paid job. After spending years studying Latin and Greek, Jude applies for admission to Christminster (i.e. Oxford) University, and receives a reply from the arch-villain of the piece, the principal of Biblioll College:

BIBLIOLL COLLEGE

SIR, – I have read your letter with interest; and judging from your description of yourself as a working-man, I venture to think that you will have a much better chance of success in life by remaining in your own sphere and sticking to your trade than by adopting any other course. That, therefore, is what I advise you to do. Yours faithfully,

T. TETUPHENAY

This is more or less exactly the view that contemporary English governments appear to hold. Certainly, where non-university students are concerned, it is to people's 'own sphere' (and current workplace) that they direct government money and subsidy. They do now provide financial aid and support for all and any young full-time students who wish to attend university, and especially for those from poorer families. In further education, by contrast, provision for anyone over eighteen is increasingly and almost exclusively 'vocational' in the narrow sense.

The development of rational thought and the support of inquiry and learning without any immediate economic applications are most often associated with universities. Since logical and critical, let alone original, thinking are very difficult, this is understandable. But it does not mean that education for non-vocational purposes and the development of reason are confined to, or even uniquely suited to, universities (Graham, 2005; Wolf, 2007a; Rose, 2002). In fact, historically, the institutions that have been most dedicated to this end, rather than to preparing their students for lucrative employment, have been the girls' secondary schools of the nineteenth century, before the job market opened up for women, and bodies such as the working men's colleges of the industrial cities, which were dedicated to bringing general and liberal education to employed men (and women). The ideals still live on in some of these colleges, but there is less and less public funding available for this purpose.

The role of government

But surely, one might argue, if people want liberal education, they should just pay for it? Now that we are so much richer than our Victorian forebears, is there any argument for directly subsidising forms of educational provision that are not primarily an investment designed to produce future income? In the latter case, as was argued above, there may be problems of uncertainty and risk which make people nervous about committing funds and so lead to underinvestment. But in the case of post-compulsory education which is undertaken because of its intrinsic content and interest, it is surely obvious to people almost at once whether they are receiving the benefits they wanted. And if they are not, they can move on.

There are, in fact, a number of arguments, both theoretical and practical, that can be advanced for subsidising post-compulsory and adult education which is undertaken entirely or partly for purposes other than enhancing productivity. The theoretical arguments relate to the possibility of individual ignorance and to both individual and social benefits. The practical arguments involve the negative consequences of attempting to draw fine distinctions between the purposes of one form of education as compared with another, and the problems of ensuring high-quality provision without 'income smoothing' and institutional support. Let us start with theory.

Why might one subsidise 'education for its own sake'?

Governments frequently force, nudge or tempt people into doing things that they might not do freely, on the grounds that these are good for them, society as a whole or both. Libertarians tend to dislike this (in part because governments can all too easily acquire a taste for it, intervening on the slightest excuse and doing more harm than good) (see Myddelton, 2007). For example, most people would accept that, because children lack the ability to reason fully, there is a case for making sure that they receive an education; but forcing people over sixteen to stay in education, as English law will shortly do, is far less justifiable (Wolf, 2008).

Subsidising general education and 'leisure classes' for adults is, however, very common across the developed world (as are subsidies for the arts), which suggests that there are some quite widespread and deep-rooted preferences and opinions underlying such subsidies. Do they have merit?

First of all, there are good reasons to suppose that education is not something people automatically have a taste for (primary school children do, but secondary schooling seems to drive it out of people). Adults do acquire the taste – there is good empirical evidence for this (see e.g. Jenkins et al., 2004) – but it is not something that comes universally or quickly. This is especially true for people whose own families were not highly educated. So one might want to make it cheaper in order to increase take-up, and help people find out what they were missing.

This is going to involve a fair number of deadweight subsidies benefiting many people who would pay anyway. But that is true for a lot of things – municipal swimming pools, opera houses, hospitals, and all those parts of the public education system that are dedicated to 'useful' learning. Any attempt to target subsidies directly according to whether people are more or less likely to be unaware of adult education's utility will be expensive, bureaucratic, arbitrary and almost certainly ineffective.

Second, there is the argument that a highly educated society is desirable for a wide variety of reasons. Some are manifestly utilitarian – that more educated societies are healthier, more tolerant and more democratic.[5] Other reasons involve the idea that education is valuable and supports other things that are valuable in and

---

5   The evidence on this is slightly mixed, especially with respect to overall levels of education and democracy, but there are certainly areas – notably health – where education influences individual behaviour, and where there are clearly knock-on effects for society as a whole (positive externalities) from improving people's health and health-related activities. For a full discussion of the evidence, see the publications of the Centre for the Wider Benefits of Learning, http://www.learningbenefits.net

of themselves: reasoned thought, culture and scholarship, for example. In other words, a society that is well educated will also be a better place all round, for everyone in it.

In order to encourage higher levels of education than will arise out of voluntary expenditures one could just rely on philanthropists like Carnegie, but that is not likely to produce either nationally available or stable provision. State subsidy could therefore be justified. These arguments are not, however, at present, popular, at least among the British political classes.

Contrast the low importance that the UK, and especially English, policy currently ascribes to anything other than an economic rationale for learning with the debates over payments for care in one's old age. In the latter case, there seems to be a feeling that any citizen should be entitled to such care for 'free', whatever their income. That this does not happen is seen as an unfortunate outcome of budgetary pressures rather than an example of policy as it should be. The idea that one should have an equivalent claim on lifelong educational access, for the health of one's mind as well as one's body, is not popular in contemporary English political argument; but it is a defensible position which has been put forward often enough in other times and places.

If one believes that high levels of education are 'good' for society, and that this is an argument for government subsidies, it is not at all obvious why this type of support should not be equally available to all citizens or only available through certain highly circumscribed institutions such as universities. Why should university degrees with a strong element of general education be highly subsidised but no subsidy be available to adults who have not gone to university, but who also wish to enlarge their minds? If this argument for subsidising post-compulsory education is accepted at all, then it applies across the board, to all forms of education, not just to those who attend a particular type of institution. And vice-versa.

Critics of subsidies for non-vocational further and adult provision very often conjure up the spectacle of taxpayers paying for middle-class basket-weaving classes. And it certainly is true that, as adult education classes have vanished over the last few years, many middle-class learners have managed to find other provision, often through the cooperative 'University of the Third Age'. What that also means is that the main losers from recent changes have been older and non-middle-class learners, who have not been able to find other opportunities, and whose numbers have fallen precipitously (see Chapter 2).

The argument for subsidising non-vocational education is a general one; it is about lowering price across the board and so increasing demand. It seems arrogantly paternalistic, as well as patently overambitious, to attempt complex fine tuning of prices and subsidies on the grounds that poorer adults are more in 'need' of education, or more ignorant of its utility. Obviously, an increase in, say, the cost of evening classes will represent a larger percentage of income for less wealthy than for more wealthy people – but the same is true of anything else, whether it is bread, cinema tickets, beer, books or summer holidays.

Policy practicalities

Of course, even if one accepts that there may be arguments for subsidising post-compulsory provision undertaken in search of 'psychic' income, the theoretical rationale is not necessarily as powerful and may imply lower levels of support than for vocationally oriented training. Practically, however, the distinction between vocational and non-vocational education is far from clear. Attempting to distinguish between them for practical policy purposes is probably impossible, and certain to be expensive, bureaucratic and wasteful.

The difficulty (and possible folly) of trying to draw fine distinctions is perhaps best explained through two examples. The first is university education. As already noted, governments have, at least so far, drawn back from trying to control what subjects universities offer.[6] In defending the value of 'non-vocational' degrees, academics can and do stress that such degrees appear, in fact, to have strong vocational pay-offs: their holders enjoy high economic returns from their education. This may be because of 'signalling': a degree indicates that its holder is bright and hard-working. But at least some of the benefits reflect skills gained while studying, including the ability to analyse, argue, express oneself and investigate a topic. More generally, there is good reason to argue that the most vocationally relevant education anyone can acquire is a general education including a mastery of the 3Rs at a relatively high level (Levy and Murnane, 2004).

The second example is 'adult basic skills'. Adult educators, when defending their patch, tend to argue for free provision of literacy instruction on the grounds that this, at least, is self-evidently 'useful' and economically productive – something with which politicians and the general public would generally agree. Unfortunately, as Box 10 explains, they are wrong. *If subsidies are*

---

6   They do offer different funding levels according to the costs of broad categories of degree, so that science, for example, is funded at higher levels than humanities; but within these broad categories, institutions are free to choose what degree titles and content to offer.

Box 10 Adult literacy

Modern societies demand literacy skills at quite a high level in an ever larger number of occupations. As such, adults with good literacy and numeracy skills consistently earn more than those without (Machin et al., 2001). So it seems obvious that adult literacy classes can be justified in economic terms, and not just because they open new horizons for people and enable them to cope better with everyday living. That has certainly been the assumption of government policy (Moser/ DfEE, 1999; DfES, 2001). Alan Wells, for many years the head of the government's adult literacy quango, and more recently a trenchant critic of its funding policies, makes precisely the same assumption, arguing that adult literacy and numeracy are 'obviously' different from other adult education courses because being functionally illiterate is economically harmful (Wells, 2008).

He is wrong: they are not, if the only criterion is the rate of return from taking such courses in adulthood. Qualifications obtained in adult life, including degrees, generally attract lower rates of return than those gained as a young person – partly, but not only, because they apply to a shorter period of someone's working life. Some adult qualifications – notably low-level vocational ones – attract no positive financial returns at all (Machin et al., 2001; Wolf et al., 2006; Jenkins et al., 2007). For basic skills, however, the results are more complex.

The large longitudinal survey that has followed the lives and careers of children born in a single week of 1958 (the National Child Development Study) has also tested participants directly at various points. It finds that people in their thirties who report that their literacy and numeracy skills have improved since they were in their teens tend to earn a little more than others, holding other relevant factors constant (education, time in work, family background, etc.). But taking a literacy or numeracy course did not seem to have any positive effects on earnings at all – if anything the opposite, although this probably reflects other characteristics of the small number who report any such activity (Machin et al., 2001).

A recent study of participants in workplace-based basic skills courses funded by the government as part of its major programme for promoting adult literacy found similarly small or non-existent financial benefits. The only participants whose literacy skills were significantly (though still quite modestly) higher a year after they started their course than before taking it were those who spoke English as a second language. And no relationship was found between measured skill improvement and reported income gains or promotion (Wolf et al., 2009). Subsidising basic skills provision for adults can be justified in a large number of ways but direct productivity gains are not one of them.

to be allocated entirely according to financial returns, adult literacy provision would bite the dust. Is that something we should applaud in a civilised society?

Whatever weight one assigns to the theoretical arguments for 'non-vocational' provision, the practical arguments against a system that differentiates are surely overwhelming. People are by far the best judges of what they want and need from education and training. Governments, by contrast, are very bad judges – indeed, if the government tries to 'pick winners' it sets itself an impossible task. It is not only impossible to weigh up the social costs and benefits of education programmes, it is impossible to distinguish in practice between vocational and non-vocational elements of general qualifications. Given the English government's record when it has decided to pick winners, and micro-manage course provision on the basis of supposed economic pay-offs (see Chapters 2 and 7), we should be very grateful that it has, so far, steered clear of attempting this at degree level.

It should therefore be entirely up to the individual which form of education and training he or she undertakes. Any subsidies should be given to the individual and whether or not a particular course can attract a subsidy should depend on how much of that individual's subsidy entitlement has been used up.[7] Subsidies for post-compulsory education should therefore make no distinctions between 'vocational' and 'leisure' activities. Abolishing the principle of subsidising courses rather than learners does not necessarily mean abolishing *all* differential subsidies. One can still, for example, accept the argument (see above) that poorer individuals have higher risk aversion and so need higher levels of subsidy – or perhaps some form of state-guaranteed loan.[8]

Summary

There are benefits from undertaking education that do not relate

---

7   As discussed below, there are various ways in which the subsidy may be allocated and administered; and no necessity for this to be a 'sudden death' affair in which people move directly from maximum to no subsidy.

8   A very large number of societies also offer higher subsidies for the unemployed (though usually only for 'vocational training') and/or subsidies for the old. This is a way of using education as a direct means of redistributing income; and also contributes to the Christmas-tree nature of most post-compulsory funding systems. These often, and not just in the UK, end up festooned with multiple special grants, and entitlements that are opaque, inefficient and administratively costly.

to increases in productivity. There are therefore worthwhile policy debates about the role of government in subsidising the provision of non-vocational courses.

Individuals may face the same problems of access to funding for non-vocational education as they face when seeking funding for vocational education. It can also be argued that the price of non-vocational further education should be reduced by subsidy because of people's ignorance of its rewards, and because of its benefits for society as a whole. In addition, and critically, it is impossible to distinguish in practice between the vocational and non-vocational elements of any form of education, and thus it is highly undesirable to discriminate between them when deciding on the degree of government support that should be provided. Attempts to do so are likely to produce massive government failure and huge bureaucracy.

Individuals should be able to use any education subsidies that are available for whatever type of education and training they please, regardless of the objective imputed to it by others.

7 ENGLAND'S POST-COMPULSORY EDUCATION AND TRAINING SECTOR: EVALUATING CURRENT ARRANGEMENTS

Earlier in this monograph, the chaotic inefficiency of our current system of post-compulsory education and training was described in some detail. This chapter revisits current arrangements from a more theoretical perspective. How far do our arrangements for funding and provision reflect the principles outlined in previous chapters? And how far do they represent a totally different approach from the one I have argued for?

Summary of the argument so far

To evaluate the system overall, let us recapitulate the conclusions of previous chapters, though in a somewhat different order. These conclusions and recommendations divide into three groups: those relating to individual entitlements; the employers' role; and government activities.

Individual entitlements

- There are some good arguments for government expenditure on post-compulsory education and training. Specifically, there is a case for providing financial assistance to individuals, directly or indirectly. If people have to pay full cost, under full market conditions, a combination of risk aversion, uncertainty and credit constraints is likely to lead to significant 'under-consumption', meaning that people will undertake less education and training than would benefit them in wage terms.

- Individuals may face the same problems of access to funding for education undertaken for non-economic as for economic reasons. There are also some arguments for subsidy because of people's ignorance of the rewards of education and because of its benefits for society as a whole.

- Individuals are by far the best judges of their own interests and of the value to them of different education and training options. Individual demand should determine what the education and training system provides and any subsidies that individuals receive should be theirs to use as they please. There should be no distinctions on the basis of objectives imputed to the learning by others.

- People's demonstrable willingness to pay for education and training that they value underscores the case for a subsidy of – but not total payment for – post-compulsory education and training undertaken for career reasons. Such a subsidy will reduce the prices (and risks) people face at the margin and so increase uptake.

- These arguments apply generally and inclusively: by level and institution of study (university, FE, workplace) and by content.

The employer's role

- Taxpayers should not be involved in subsidising employers by paying for workplace activity that includes large amounts of firm-specific training.

- Individual employees, like all adult citizens, face the problems of risk and uncertainty and access to capital discussed earlier. In many cases, the workplace may be the appropriate venue for acquiring the skills. Funding should nonetheless be channelled through the individual and reach employers only via individuals' decisions and commitments.

- Governments need, in this context, to address labour market regulation so as to allow a wider variety of agreements between employers and employees who wish to acquire skills in the workplace and on the job. The cost of training may often be financed by wage reductions.

- Apprenticeships should be thought of as part of the general education system, not as part of on-the-job training, and should be subsidised on the same grounds as other forms of post-compulsory education. They are appropriate for specific occupations, and require intensive employer involvement.

- Employers who offer apprenticeships may require payments over and above the fees they receive from the apprentices because apprenticeship is appropriately conceptualised as part of the education system, not as part of an enterprise's in-house training.

The government's role

- There is no reason why governments should only concern themselves with the economic outcomes of post-compulsory education. Non-economic benefits from education should also be considered by policymakers and 'market failure' is possible in this area too. Market failure, however, does not necessarily produce an unanswerable argument for government intervention.

- The practical difficulties of discriminating between different types of educational outcome are overwhelming and likely to produce massive government failure. This difficulty alone is enough to rule out as undesirable and inefficient any subsidy programme which attempts to differentiate between 'desirable' and 'undesirable' outcomes and motives for undertaking learning. Individuals should be able to use whatever subsidies are generally available for whatever type of education and training they please, regardless of the objective imputed to it by others.

- Governments have a useful role to play in ensuring that potential and current learners have access to good information. They will be less able to perform this function if they are involved in direct provision and in promoting some types of qualification or programme over others.

- Governments have a role to play in providing, maintaining and policing the legal infrastructure for the provision of education and training to individuals, including ensuring that labour market regulation does not militate against training arrangements between individuals and employers, and that individuals have ready recourse against incompetent or fraudulent providers. Their single most important task, however, is to provide credit and risk-spreading institutions that enable individuals to avail themselves of the opportunities they are offered.

- There is nothing whatsoever in the recent history or current delivery of education and training which suggests that governments will be better able than individuals to see the future, and overcome uncertainty. The contrary is true.

Relationship between further and higher education

Because current practice in the two sectors is so very different, it is worth underlining the following points.

- There is no reason on 'human capital' grounds to justify providing those students who are building up human capital full-time in universities with consistently more generous assistance than part-time undergraduates, apprentices or students in further education colleges, private colleges and training establishments.
- This follows from the more general point that there is no argument for treating citizens differently with respect to subsidies according to how they study and where.[1] On the contrary: the economic arguments imply non-differentiation by subject, mode of study, institutional type and individual. The economic arguments also imply freedom for learners to choose where, when and what they learn.

To summarise the principles for fair and efficient funding in this way is to demonstrate how far our current system departs

---

1   How far students' entitlements should be related to their own current or familial circumstances is a moot point. If government assistance offsets the problems created by risk and credit constraints, it is not clear why further selective subsidies should be needed; but conversely, as discussed above, a sizeable body of opinion argues that poorer people are, very rationally, more risk averse and so need more help. The latter argument has been accepted in the design of university student funding, but there is no definitive empirical answer; the decision will ultimately be political.

from them. Fifteen points are made relating to how provision should be organised. They include the statement that governments have a case for providing some subsidies or other support (such as guaranteed loans) to individuals for general education and training; and governments do indeed provide these. There is also a case for some support to employers providing apprenticeships, and governments provide this too. None of the other principles outlined above, however, is followed in practical policy. Even the two sound economic principles that are followed are only partially implemented. Assistance to individuals is distributed in an enormously inequitable fashion, and only some classes of citizen are entitled to subsidies for courses that are not avowedly aimed at enhancing skills and productivity.

As Chapter 2 demonstrated, our current system is also extraordinarily complex. One reason for this is, of course, that it departs to such an extent from sound underlying principles. This leads to continual and visible failures and a continual policy activism to try to improve matters. The failure of policy to achieve what it should is addressed through yet more initiatives of the same sort: more quangos, more rules and regulations, more detailed control of colleges' actions and of what they can teach, more attempts to forecast the labour market of the future and its 'needs'. The remainder of this chapter highlights the major respects in which funding principles and current practice diverge.

The provision of individual entitlements

There are strong reasons for providing general subsidies for further and adult education, and also for ensuring that decisions about participation should rest with the individual. That implies a policy of simply changing the price facing all would-be learners through a straightforward individual subsidy entitlement.

At present, there is no equitable provision of entitlements to all citizens. Entitlements for and within that subset of the population which wins a full-time undergraduate place at university are clear and well understood. But for part-time students, as for all students in further education (FE), there is a complex mix of much smaller grants and subsidies. Their constantly changing nature is of itself a barrier to rational decision-making by learners or providers of education and training.

Second, subsidies should be general and across the board and not tied to specific courses or modes of learning. It should then be left to individuals whether further education is pursued with those subsidies. This has generally been the case with core parts of university education, where subsidies are available to every (EU) citizen who is able to secure a place on a course at a recognised British university (with no limits on how often one applies). At undergraduate level, all students in England and Wales pay a sizeable proportion of their degree costs; at the same time, a mechanism is in place, at least for full-timers, that addresses risk and uncertainty issues (income-contingent loans are offered through the Student Loans Company). Of course, students must meet relevant entry conditions. Nothing in this argument precludes substantive conditions that ensure people only enter programmes for which they are qualified: entry on to a programme should be a matter of agreement between the learner and the provider.

British universities are placed under pressure to increase their intake of students from non-independent schools, and must submit plans to show they are developing access policies. Until this year, however, there was no mandatory differentiated pricing for a given degree on the basis of student characteristics or direct control of admissions decisions. There are various limits on the number of places given to students to study different courses at undergraduate level, though not at postgraduate level (at which there is no general entitlement to subsidy). For 2009/10, however, the government has also introduced rules limiting funding for degrees where the student already has an 'equivalent level qualification' (no matter when obtained, or in what field). The institutions most affected by this have been the Open University and Birkbeck, which specialise in adult students, many of whom are changing careers and returning to the labour market.

Part-timers are much less well served: there is a policy of differential subsidies for part-timers compared with full-timers, and also for postgraduate as opposed to undergraduate students.[2]

Even with these changes, funding for university study remains relatively clear as well as generous. In further education, however, a highly complex web of entitlements and subsidy patterns has existed for many years. Whether or not any subsidy is paid, and how much, varies according to people's age and financial and employment/benefit status. Again, these rules change constantly.

Subsidy patterns mean that, in practice, FE, adult education and workplace students either have access to 100 per cent subsidies (free courses) and courses for which only very small fees are levied; *or* can only attend courses for which they have to pay all costs. It is hard to think of any circumstances under which this could lead to a result that is remotely efficient – that is, the best

---

2   Extending full-timers' entitlements to part-timers, at undergraduate level, and for home students only, would cost about £250 million per annum in grants and the same in loan payments. HC Deb, 28 April 2008, column 112W: answer by Bill Rammell to tabled question.

outcome is achieved for a given amount of funding provided by the state.

One hundred per cent subsidies limit enormously the volume of subsidised provision available from a given budget, as well as making it highly arbitrary whether a particular individual gets everything or nothing. Moreover, there is no reason to suppose, on theoretical or practical grounds, that 100 per cent subsidies are necessary in order to promote take-up of valued skills. (Think of how many people pay for their own driving lessons.) Of course, if what is being offered is not highly rated by individual learners, they may very well, and quite rationally, be unwilling to contribute; conversely, if they were contributing to the cost of courses there would be incentives to drive up the quality of provision.

Although most discussion focuses on the cost of courses and on fees (since these determine institutions' incomes), for learners themselves, living costs are at least as important. Here, too, there is no clear, uniform system, and certainly nothing even approaching equity between higher and further education. Table 5 shows expenditure on student support for further and higher education over the period 2007–09. Even without the bursaries now being paid out directly by universities, the contrast is dramatic.

Differentiation by type of learning

Previous chapters argued against the idea that subsidies should vary by the imputed objective of learning. Outside the universities, the current system takes the opposite view. The Secretary of State's grant letter of 2008/09 to the Learning and Skills Council (LSC) emphasises that 'Funds must continue to be aligned to our

Table 5 **Government expenditures on student support (maintenance and non-fee costs): higher and further education, England, 2007–09**

Category	2007/08	2008/09 (est.)
Further education: support to learners 19+	£ million	£ million
Career Development Loans	21	50
Adult Learning Grant	18	30
Learner support: '19+ hardship' (allocated and paid out by colleges)	42	44
Childcare for workless families	33	35
Other misc. support	13	8
Total	**127**	**167**
Higher education: support to learners 19+	£ million	£ million
Student maintenance loans	2,631	2,541
Student maintenance grants	1,080	1,198
Access funds and bursaries (central government)	52	50
Bursaries to individuals, awarded by universities, using mandated part of fee income	192	192
Total	**3,955**	**3,981**

Sources: Annual reports and accounts, LSC; Annual reports, DIUS; Student Support for Higher Education in England, Statistical First Release 2008/9 (Student Loan Company and DIUS); Learner Support Progress Report and Issues, Internal paper ref. LSC 26/2008 (Learning and Skills Council)

key priorities'. This applies to the content of courses, the skills developed and to the types and level of qualification.

English governments' determination to control the type of learning that people undertake, using funding mechanisms as their primary tool, is far wider-reaching and more detailed in execution than in any other country of which I am aware (including Scotland). Under the Conservative governments of

Box 11 Eligibility for funding

Who is eligible for how much subsidy, and how much will be paid to providers of English education and training, depends on a web of funding formulae, regulations, special payments, incentives and restrictions, which changes almost by the month. A recent user-friendly 'Hands-on guide to post-16 funding 2008/9' (Linford, 2008) covers 'adult-learner-responsive-funding models', 'additional learning support' and its differences from 'learner support funding', new '1.92 (G) programmes', and the move from 'loadbanded base rates' to 'SLNs' (*sic*). It runs to 114 pages and was, of course, out of date within weeks. The Learning and Skills Council's own 2008/09 guidance on funding models covers 257 pages (summer 2009) and has to be read alongside a separate document on 'The Funding Formula'.

the 1980s and early 1990s, vocational education was effectively nationalised. In the case of courses leading to vocational qualifications, subsidies were made available only when those qualifications met tight government guidelines on content, format and assessment method (Wolf, 2001, 2002).

Under the Labour governments of the last decade, the linking of subsidy to content and 'type' of learning has increased enormously. An ever larger proportion of public funding is earmarked for courses that lead to formal qualifications and which are on an 'approved' list. Any courses that do not lead to formal qualifications have progressively lost support.

So-called 'leisure courses' (such as adult education courses that do not lead to qualifications) are seen as especially undeserving of public subsidy. Removal of funding from anything that anyone might be doing for the 'wrong' reason has been achieved in large part by targeting funds to courses leading to qualifications that have been placed on an approved list. Being on that list means that they have been through all the long scrutiny and approval processes organised by various of the government's quangos. This process involves, *inter alia*, judgements being made about their relevance to 'skill' promotion in a particular occupational sector.

The restrictions on what 'ought' to be studied have been further tightened by concentrating funding on 'full' awards and on certain priority qualification 'levels'. Full awards are a subset of those on the government's approved list (see Box 2, Chapter 2, above). They require either extensive periods in college, and so are taken predominantly by young people under 25 and by some older adults on benefits, or are assessed in the workplace. Differential subsidy by *levels* of award is possible because, as part of its central planning of provision, the UK has assigned every qualification that is 'approved' to a level within the 'National Qualifications Framework' (see Chapter 2). At present, Level 2s are all the rage: the LSC will provide money for those in preference to any other level. LSC figures show that the number of places on courses leading to lower-level qualifications correspondingly fell by 600,000 in 2007/08 (because the government did not fund them; not because students did not choose to take them). At the same time, not all Level 2 awards are equally favoured: GCSE Maths for adult learners, for example, is funded significantly less generously than is a Level 2 'Key Skill' in 'number'.

The most recent policy of differentiation by type of learning was mentioned above in the context of university study: namely that subsidies can be paid only for learning that takes place at a level which the learner has never before undertaken. So if someone has already attained a Level 2, or 3, or 4 qualification – no matter what the content, or how long ago – they cannot receive any further subsidy for another qualification at that level. They can only be subsidised for a course, leading to a qualification, which is at a higher level than they have previously achieved. This restriction was at first applied at all levels of the post-compulsory system, and clearly militates against any form of retraining or career change.

More recently, in a rush to spend Train to Gain money, the restriction was lifted for that programme, while being retained everywhere else. At the time of writing, an individual can be signed up for accreditation with a Level 2 in the workplace, through Train to Gain, whether they have one, two or indeed six Level 2s already. They will be refused any form of subsidy, however, let alone a free place, for the same award if they want to study for it in college, and already hold any 'Level 2'. Thus somebody who has lost their job, for whom the risks and lack of credit may be greater, will not have access to funding to train for a qualification in a new field at the same level as qualifications they already hold. On the other hand, somebody who already has a job may well have access to funding.

The most far-reaching mechanism of all for dividing 'approved' from 'non-approved' learning is the requirement that all qualifications offered in the sector, other than in universities, must have gone through central validation and approval and have been placed on a master list; and the practice of funding only 'qualification-bearing' courses. Qualifications' content, structure, assessment, level, time (notionally) required to attain them, and economic relevance must all be determined, scrutinised and agreed by four separate bodies for vocational awards and three for general educational ones.

Overall, far from thinking that individuals are the best judges of their own interests, successive governments have been convinced that the vast majority of adult citizens (unlike eighteeen-year-old A-level candidates) must be treated as children and told exactly what is good for them. Universities, in comparison, continue to enjoy considerable autonomy and have been able to change their course offerings, develop new markets and, indeed, increase their contacts with and contracts from employers. Universities award their own degrees, although they do now have to undergo audit by the Quality Assurance Agency; and there is no attempt to decide, from outside, what is a worthy 'vocational' degree and what is a pariah 'leisure' pursuit.

The employer

This monograph has argued strongly that funding should go to individuals and not to businesses: there are good arguments for subsidising the former, none for the latter. In practice, as discussed earlier, government policy has been the diametrical opposite: to fund businesses, with individuals obtaining training only through their employer, in their role as employees. The nature of this funding, however, has failed to assist employers to carry out the one key education and training role for which state subsidy can be justified – namely apprenticeship training.

The current government's flagship training programme, 'Train to Gain', has received considerable attention in this monograph. Its purpose is encapsulated in its title, and its major supporter, outside government, has been, not surprisingly, the

CBI. In questioning the rationale for providing direct subsidies to existing companies, we have queried whether it was the job of governments to bolster the position of established companies and market leaders vis-à-vis small companies and future entrants into a market. Box 12 underscores the large amounts of money being allocated to some of the largest companies in the UK (which are also, of course, able to contribute large numbers of qualifications or 'attainments' to the targets that dominate public sector programmes).

In Chapter 2, we noted the general, and to ministers surprising, lack of enthusiasm for Train to Gain, and the difficulty providers were experiencing in finding employers to accept this 'free' training. In large part this is because it is not actually training, let alone customised training, which they are being offered. Because large companies also have large in-house training programmes, however, it is much easier for them than for small companies to integrate Train to Gain activities with their pre-existing training programmes and, therefore, to obtain direct benefit from it. Indeed, some companies have been encouraged, by government, to become 'awarding bodies' and award (and be paid for awarding) qualifications directly. Note, however, that these are not qualifications that have been developed in response to *individuals'* demands and choices. On the contrary: public funding goes directly to the companies, so that they can 'deliver' qualifications that meet government's current priorities. The driver behind recognition of companies' existing training programmes as 'qualification-bearing' is, once again, the wish to meet quantitative targets embedded in Public Service Agreements (PSAs).

This is not the only way in which current policy with respect to employers is totally misconceived, however. At the same time as

Box 12 Train to Gain expenditures

In 2007/08, contracts worth more than £200,000 included:

- £722,750 to BUPA Care Homes Ltd
- £543,000 to Rentokil Initial 1927 plc
- £455,200 to the Ford Motor Company Limited

In 2006/07, individual payments over £200,000 accounted for 18 per cent of disbursements. Recipients included:

- McDonald's Restaurants Ltd £910,000
- Peugeot Citroën Automobiles UK Limited £526,665
- BP Oil UK Limited £465,105

In 2005/06, payments over £200,000 accounted for £10,541,000 in total and included:

- £1,184,000 to First Group plc
- £585,000 to Alfred McAlpine plc
- £403,000 to Royal Mail group plc
- £282,500 to Kwik-Fit (GB) Ltd

Source: LSC, Freedom of Information request response, ref 06–08–2008–153421–002

funnelling ever larger proportions of the post-compulsory budget into workplace activity of doubtful value, governments have paid lip-service to the idea of apprenticeships while developing policies that militate against the creation of successful ones. Apprenticeships should sit firmly within a particular firm and large firms are often in a good position to deliver high-quality apprenticeships. Paradoxically, however, providing funding to deliverers of training rather than to students themselves has led to a situation where apprenticeships are often taking place away from the workplace and within special training organisations. This problem is exacerbated by the bureaucratic control of apprenticeship courses.

A good deal has been written about the current state of apprenticeship in the UK.[3] Briefly, the core problem is that large numbers of programmes have been labelled 'apprenticeships' which are in fact no such thing; while the regulation and centralised planning of apprenticeship content and delivery have become so detailed and onerous as to make it very difficult indeed for employers, as opposed to full-time training companies, to offer them.

Like everything else in this sector, apprenticeships have targets attached to them, and allowing ministers to proclaim 'success by numbers' is the main driver of day-to-day policy. All and any programmes designed for young people who dislike or are unsuccessful in academic settings, and which emphasise practical experience, have been labelled 'apprenticeships'.

Often, current British apprenticeships purport to be offering training and experience in the workplace while hardly involving employers at all. This is because much of the current Modern Apprenticeship programme involves training providers whose 'industry' is simply the provision of apprenticeships. Young people can often complete an 'apprenticeship' on the basis of some short work placements with employers who have no major

---

3   See, for example, House of Lords Economic Affairs Committee (2007), Fuller and Unwin (2003, 2008), Ryan and Unwin (2001).

involvement with the programme or, indeed, no real workplace experience at all.[4]

It is actually much easier to deliver apprenticeships in line with government regulations – and to collect your 'outcome-related funding' once the apprentices have completed their qualifications – if you are a full-time 'training provider'. First, the whole programme is tightly linked to highly specific and detailed content requirements, developed by the government-established network of Sector Skill Councils, and linked to centrally written and approved qualifications (NVQs) with onerous requirements for assessment and recording of multiple practical operations. These are completely uniform even though the hallmarks of the modern workplace are variability, continual change and speciali-sation. Second, the bureaucratic and record-keeping requirements are onerous. They are much easier to cope with if such activities are the core business; they are also subject to economies of scale.

One result is that inspectors' verdicts on quality are at complete odds with the verdicts of the labour market. Detailed studies of inspection reports on apprenticeships show that government inspectors give much lower ratings, on average, to apprenticeships actually run by employers (all of them large companies) than to those run by training companies (see Ryan et al., 2007; Lewis and Ryan, 2009a). Yet it is apprentices with

4   The nature of many current apprenticeships explains why, at the same time as total numbers have been expanding, numbers at Level 3 (craft) fell from 60,000 funded places for those under nineteen and 103,000 for those nineteen and over in 2002 to 51,000 and 97,000 in 2004/05. In 2005, only 25,000 16–18 year olds started Level 3 apprenticeships, compared with 80,000 at lower levels. 'Programme-led' apprenticeships, which are essentially employer-led, were 9 per cent of total starts in 2005 and down to 6.5 per cent of total apprenticeship starts in 2007/08 (Hansard, 8 May 2009, column 476W; 25 January 2006, column 2192W; and 22 April 2009, column 740W).

companies who are much more likely to get jobs at the end of their training. Families and young people know this: it is the company-based schemes which are hugely oversubscribed. But for government bureaucrats and funding agencies, it is the inspection reports which carry weight.

All of this makes our so-called 'apprenticeship' programme comprehensively different from that of other, successful systems. It also underlines the comprehensive misalignment between current government policy and the principles outlined above for effective employer involvement in educating the young.

The government

The government's role should be to address very specific problems that might exist with the purely private finance of further education. This includes problems caused by risk and uncertainty. The problems can be addressed by improving the availability and quality of information on education and training; by making credit available to those who are creditworthy but who may not be able to access private credit markets except at very high interest rates; by using a combination of across-the-board subsidy at the point of purchase and subsidised insurance against the inability to repay loans; and by ensuring that learners have recourse against incompetent (or fraudulent) providers. In the post-compulsory sector, governments carry out these tasks reasonably well with respect to higher education, for full-time undergraduate students, through income-contingent loans, bursaries and grants, and subsidies paid directly to universities. Part-time students and graduates are not treated in a consistent or equitable fashion even within higher education; while in the rest of the post-compulsory sector, government fails utterly to carry out these basic tasks while attempting, instead, to plan provision and deliver it.

Politicians and civil servants have repeatedly rejected the idea that they cannot 'pick winners' and plan the system. The most recent in a string of official reports is the Leitch report, commissioned by then Chancellor Gordon Brown and currently driving government policy and expenditure in post-compulsory education and training (including, to some degree, higher education). Its author, Lord Leitch, was requested to identify the 'optimal level of skills in the economy' for the country, a task he accepted without demur and announced that he had achieved (Leitch, 2006: 15, para. 38). He also, memorably, informed the government that: 'History tells us that no one can predict with any accuracy future occupational skills. The Review is clear that skill demands will increase at every single level' (ibid.: 13, para. 29).

Successive governments have been completely unwilling to accept that adult individuals can and should be the best judges of their own economic prospects, and of the education and training they undertake for economic and other purposes. On the one hand, they are convinced that 'needs' are not being met; that people should be nudged towards engineering, or computer programming, by providing greater subsidies to these favoured fields. On the other, they find it intolerable to think that subsidies may make something they disapprove of cheaper. Outside universities, subsidies are highly selective: individuals must on no account receive subsidies to help them study philosophy, or drama, or Chinese instead of the 'right' courses for themselves and the economy.[5] Overall, we have had twenty years of cumulatively

5 Among seven-year-olds, however, studying French or Chinese is apparently highly desirable, on economic grounds. At present, foreign language teaching is

more detailed central planning of provision: as Box 13 shows, the Leitch report provides excellent examples, but they are in a direct line from predecessors.

The rationale for this far-reaching and ambitious engineering of what adults learn is frequently reiterated by ministers. It is that, left to itself, the country, and the post-compulsory system, will not produce the skills that the economy needs. As discussed in Chapter 2, training policy has, under Labour, been the government's preferred mechanism for increasing productivity, and it retains total faith that this can happen: according to the Leitch report, which it commissioned and accepted, meeting the quantitative targets currently set would mean that: 'The rate of productivity growth would increase by at least 10 per cent, helping to close the UK's productivity gap' (Leitch, 2006: 15, para. 42).

Yet, as discussed above, to date, *none of the expected and planned-for increases in productivity growth has materialised.* The lower-level, vocational awards to which ever-increasing parts of government subsidy are tied produce, at best, extremely modest increases in their holders' incomes; and the 'NVQ Level 2s', which are the government's best beloved, are associated with either no increase at all in incomes or, in many studies, with an actual fall (see e.g. Dearden et al., 2004; Wolf et al., 2006; Jenkins et al., 2007; Wolf, 2008). Table 6 below reproduces a typical set of results, as published by one of the government's own quangos, the Sector Skills Development Agency.

---

a high priority for primary schools. Secondary pupils, however, are not required to study a language to GCSE, and among adults, language learning is derided as a 'leisure' pursuit for which no public support can possibly be justified.

Box 13 The Leitch report

The Leitch report (2006) is full of detailed recommendations for amendments to and improvements in the post-compulsory education and training system. These give a clear indication of the latter's highly centralised and complex nature before the most recent changes, and additional centralisation and complexity thereafter. To give just a few examples:

There will remain four key elements of a national framework. First, the Government will identify priorities for investment of public funds. Second, the LSC will only fund programmes leading to qualifications approved by SSCs. Third, the LSC will work to ensure quality by identifying providers that can receive public funds – this process should ensure that all providers of good quality are accredited. Fourth, the LSC will act to promote effective competition. (4.17)

Each Department must measure the contribution of each of its agencies to the sustainable employment and progression of their customers. (7.65)

The contribution of each Department is outlined in its Public Service Agreements (PSAs). The DfES* should continue to be held accountable for improving skills and delivering qualifications through the new PSA framework, with the volumes set out in Chapter 3. It ... should require skills providers to measure the employment and pay prospects of a representative sample of those completing courses over a three year period, similar to the approach already taken by some universities. The DWP should be held accountable through the PSA framework for improving the employment rate over the cycle. (7.66)

The Review recommends strengthening the voice of employers through the creation of a single, employer-led Commission for Employment and Skills to deliver leadership and influence within a national framework of individual rights and responsibilities. (8.11)

The Commission will monitor whether Jobcentre Plus is making its full contribution to sustainable employment and progression. (7.68)

*In the three years since publication this job has passed to first DIUS (when DfES was broken into two) and then DBIS (into which DIUS was merged).

Table 6 **Average returns to Level 1 and 2 vocational qualifications in the UK, by gender: full-time employees of working age**

	Males (per cent)	Females (per cent)
Level 1 vocational	–4.8	–4.0
Level 2 vocational	–3.2	–5.4

Source: Dickerson (2008)[6] (adapted from Table 5, 'Controls: age, age squared, ethnicity, industry, public sector, firm size, apprenticeship, other qualifications, year dummies')

And there is no evidence that there has been any impact on 'skills shortages' as measured by repeated employer surveys.[7]

The government's function of producing better information flows has, meanwhile, been not so much abandoned as traduced. Far from admitting (let alone publicising) the limitations of current policy, governments have been engaged in wholesale denial (punctuated by attempts to reanalyse yet another data set in search of different findings). Rather than providing accurate and objective comparisons of options, they dedicate large sums

6   These results use data from the Labour Force Survey (pooled for 2000–04), and the estimated rates of return can be cumulated (Dickerson, 2008: 8). Some other analyses use data from one of the detailed cohort surveys. The advantage of the former is that they cover the whole working population, but they track individuals only for a short period. The cohort studies are longitudinal, but look only at those born in 1958, or in 1970.

7   These measures are, in fact, of fairly limited worth, since any full-employment economy will be marked by skill shortages; and depressions by their absence. Nonetheless, one might expect that, at the very least, certain highly localised and specific shortages would have been addressed. A short look at the history of recent construction projects indicates otherwise. The government's central planning, which includes an apprenticeship programme with hundreds of thousands of places, has not even been able to create construction apprenticeships for East London – where there is huge demand from young people – which will allow any of them to complete craft apprenticeships before the 2012 Olympics are over and gone, let alone in time to work on the Olympic site. See written answer from Tessa Jowell, MP: HC Deb, 27 March 2008, column 368W.

of money to publicising and marketing qualifications they have recently created, at the expense of other established options (see Chapter 2). Indeed, direct government involvement in subsidising particular types of further education provision means that it is simply not in a position to provide objective information about the value of different education and training pathways.

As discussed above, the current government does a reasonably good job of providing credit and insurance for a subset of the post-compulsory population. Full-time undergraduates – who are almost all young and who are overwhelmingly middle-class – have access to income-contingent loans with subsidised interest rates. Maintenance grants and bursaries are also available to many; indeed, one of Prime Minister Brown's first actions, on taking office, was to extend enormously the number of young people eligible for maintenance grants. No such provision was made for part-timers, apprentices or FE students, although the FE budget was duly raided when the department discovered that it had grossly underestimated the cost of this change. And finally, far from promoting labour market laws and regulations that would make it easier for individuals to enter into training contracts with individual employers, the last ten years have seen a marked increase in the extent to which uniform conditions of service are incorporated into pay settlements, albeit only for the public sector (see Bach, 2009).

Overall, current policies seem dedicated as much to erecting direct barriers to individual learning as about creating the conditions that maximise it. These prevent people fulfilling their desire (and the economy's 'need') to learn new skills, especially at a time when economic upheaval is forcing many to change occupations and careers; and reduce the ability of institutions to respond to learners' preferences. The current system is opaque, wasteful, unjust, fails to achieve its own narrow economic objectives, and is effectively unreformable. Where should we go next?

8 GOVERNMENT PROVISION FOR FURTHER AND ADULT EDUCATION – A NEW MODEL

Chapter 1 argued that public subsidies for post-compulsory education and training should go primarily and directly to individuals. Furthermore, the amount of subsidy should not be affected by the nature or supposed purpose of the education and training undertaken.[1] This chapter looks at the different ways in which this might be done. It is not concerned with how much money is made available in total or how much is provided to individuals to subsidise their education and training. Rather, it looks at the type of subsidy that is most compatible with the mechanisms of individual choice recommended above and with achieving the maximum benefit from any given amount of government money that is spent. In summary, this chapter will argue that:

- Subsidies for long and short courses have to be organised and administered separately.

---

1   A caveat is needed. At the time of writing, and in common with most of the world, compulsory education ends for all British young people in their mid-teens. Also in common with most of the developed world, however, the large majority of young people currently stay in full-time education until age seventeen or eighteen. In principle, there is no reason why education and training funding during this early post-compulsory period should not be treated in exactly the same way as for older age groups. This is beyond the scope of this monograph, however, so the discussion that follows should be taken as applying to anyone of eighteen and over.

- Subsidies for all long courses should be provided on the same terms, whether they are based inside or outside universities.
- Subsidies for short courses should be paid to individuals via some form of learning account administered by a new regulated institution, organised on principles similar to the Charities Aid Foundation.[2]

One of the implications of the proposed reforms is that many forms of direct government support for courses and institutions, together with related quangos, will be abolished. This will lead either to money being saved by the government or will release money for direct support to students. The final section of this chapter looks briefly at the sums of money that could easily be released in this way, and at methods of controlling costs under a demand-driven system.

The structure of subsidy programmes

Chapter 3 concluded that there were some genuine grounds for providing subsidies to individuals undertaking post-compulsory education and training, thus lowering its price and increasing uptake. These grounds included mitigating the problems of risk and uncertainty; the lack of availability of capital; the presence of ignorance; and, possibly, the social benefits from a more educated citizenry. Individuals, I argued, are the best judges of what education and training they should undertake. Governments, conversely, are very bad judges indeed of what people 'should' learn at post-compulsory level. The main form of further

---

2   The analogy was pointed out to me by John Harwood, and is acknowledged with gratitude.

education subsidy should therefore be one that changes the price individuals pay for education and training courses and of activities that they, individually, select and for which they enrol. There may be a case for offering different individuals higher or lower subsidies, but there is no good case for tying subsidy levels to the purpose of the learning people undertake. There may also be cases where some money has to be paid directly to providers (notably employers offering apprenticeships) in order to 'smooth' income or finance infrastructure, but these should be seen as exceptions that need justifying as a special case.

Learning credits or subsidies for individuals can take a limited number of forms.

- Cash/guarantees to institutions that provide individuals with courses.
- A 'virtual' voucher – i.e. a system whereby an individual enrols in a programme, the institution registers this, and cash is then handed to the institution.
- Tax credits to individuals undertaking courses.
- A voucher that is handed over by an individual to a provider of education and training which redeems it for cash.
- Cash to the individual (with strings attached).

All these mechanisms directly reduce the price that an individual pays for learning. All these mechanisms are compatible with a system in which provision is decided directly by individuals' own choices and decisions. All of them are also compatible with *any level of subsidy*, with the individual covering the balance of costs from their own resources, and with *'banded' subsidies* (higher for some categories of recipient). They also vary substantially, however, in the degree to which they create a direct, rather than a bureaucratically mediated, link between learner and provider, and the degree to which they encourage new entrants (suppliers). I will also argue that different types of learning are more or less well suited to different forms of credit.

(A) Institutional cash and 'virtual' vouchers

The first two approaches on the list – institutional support and 'virtual' vouchers – are alike in that the subsidy comes to the supplier of learning without the learner handing it over in any direct way. Alongside this, learners may or may not pay fees, but if they do, the fees will come from their own resources.

At its simplest, institutional support involves the government handing money over to an institution such as a college to put on whatever courses that institution thinks learners (customers) will want, while charging less than full cost for these. Any government that provides such support – normally labelled a 'block grant' – is more or less bound to require that the institution meet minimum levels of provision in return, whether in terms of learners enrolled, or courses provided, or total hours spent by learners in contact with instructors. In other words, no institution, in the modern world, will readily be allowed to take a large sum of taxpayers' money, spend it on generous salaries, and enrol/teach no, or almost no, students. But beyond the minimum, it will be up to the institution how it allocates its subsidies across courses, what (top-up) fees it charges for what, and what courses it decides to offer.

Prospective students then have a choice among whatever courses the recipient institutions offer. If an institution gets this

– their 'product mix' – wrong, and students do not turn up, or pay up, it will at best suffer reduced income, and have to rethink its programme to respond better to market demand, and/or cut staff. At worst, it will fail to meet the minimum provision standards and suffer penalties (lower levels of subsidy next year, imposed management changes by central government, forced merger with a more successful institution). Overall, student demand will drive provision; and students will face lower prices because of the subsidies.

This is, historically and today, a perfectly standard approach to subsidising post-compulsory education; it has vanished from England, but was practised here recently. Scotland operates under a system of this type at present; so do institutions as diverse as community colleges in many US states,[3] and adult learning circles in Sweden.

The major problem with institutional subsidies is that they make it very difficult for new institutions to start up. Governments will hardly subsidise new entrants without a track record; but without subsidies, how can new entrants compete? A combination of institutional subsidies and (reasonable) autonomy is generally found in systems that are entirely public; and existing institutions, naturally and predictably, oppose new entrants. In the USA, for example, community colleges have vociferously and generally successfully lobbied against subsidies for private (proprietary) vocational training institutions. Barriers to entry are especially important when an institution is effectively a local monopolist, as is often the case with an FE college, as compared with a university.

---

3   US community colleges are organised by individual states, and vary greatly in their funding regimes.

In addition, governments are very bad at leaving well alone. The last twenty years in England provide vivid evidence of this, as the level of control over what should be offered, to whom, at what prices, and with what form of delivery has been ratcheted up and up. It is in the nature of funders to interfere in how their funds are spent; but a form of subsidy that involves payments to a limited number of institutions, all of which are highly dependent on these funds, makes it very easy and very tempting to interfere constantly. Other forms of subsidy make this much harder.

'Virtual vouchers' also involve payments directly to institutions, but are tied more closely to the decision of an individual student to enrol. The more who enrol, the more money the institution receives, in a direct one-to-one relationship. Fees may or may not be charged in addition: if so, they will be paid directly from the learner's own resources.

The much-studied and praised German apprenticeship system is of this type. Apprenticeship is a major destination not only for seventeen-year-olds, but also for somewhat older entrants. If you want to be an apprentice, in Germany, you start off by getting yourself an apprenticeship contract with an employer. At that point, you are, in effect, in possession of a training voucher to be realised with an educational institution, because all apprentices are entitled to a substantial amount of off-the-job training, organised, provided and paid for by the state.

Anyone with an apprenticeship contract is entitled to that training. Equally, there is no automatic entitlement to an apprenticeship: the current English apprenticeship 'entitlement' is possible only because most of our so-called apprenticeships are no such thing. There may be supply constraints in some sectors and regions so that young Germans do not get the apprenticeship they most want (just as many UK students do not get their preferred university course). But the system is clearly and simply demand-led, with young people looking for and choosing desirable apprenticeships, and the training institutions receiving students to the degree that particular apprenticeships were chosen by local people.

This form of subsidy is also common (but by no means universal) in university systems, and in school systems that operate with some degree of parent choice (where normally, as in England, additional fees on top of the payments are forbidden: subsidy is 100 per cent). A school system in which money, to a substantial degree, follows the child has now become so familiar in England that it is almost taken for granted; but it is by no means universal. Its rationale is the core 'choice and markets' argument: if 'consumers' are able to choose, then responsive, high-quality providers will be rewarded, and, overall, quality will be driven up. How far this is the case depends, among other things, on how far there are supply constraints.[4] Systems of this type will involve a list of approved recipients, and can be more or less open to new entrants. Barriers to entry are, however, lower than in the case of direct block payments to institutions.

(B) Tax credits and voucher systems

Tax credits were first proposed a long time ago, by Thomas Paine, author of *The Rights of Man*, who is sometimes, for that reason,

---

4   For example: can successful schools expand? What happens if schools become very small through loss of pupils? Are some children unable to travel, and so faced with no effective choice, and left more disadvantaged compared with their peers than before?

proclaimed as the first 'voucher' advocate. Paine did not share most of his contemporaries' and successors' conviction that the world is full of ignorant and uncaring parents who do not know the value of education and cannot be trusted to secure it for their children. His was a simple and straightforward proposal, based essentially on direct remission of taxes, though concerned with schools rather than older students and trainees.

Although a considerable number of countries offer employers tax credits for training, offering tax credits to individuals has been rather uncommon. This is partly because many of the people whom governments want to encourage into training are paying little or no tax anyway; and partly, no doubt, because it is hard to combine a tax credit of this type, claimed by the individual, with the sort of micro-management of 'acceptable' and 'desirable' education and training which modern governments have espoused in recent decades.

The 1991 Conservative government did introduce a very circumscribed credit, in the form of 'Vocational Tax Relief', which could be claimed only for activity leading to a National Vocational Qualification (a particular type of vocational qualification, sponsored by the government, and which it wanted to encourage at the expense of other vocational qualifications or non-accredited training). The annual number of claims peaked at 300,000 at a cost to the Exchequer of £60 million (House of Commons Education and Skills Committee, 2002), and it was abolished by the Labour government in 1999 to help offset the costs of a different programme, apparently without anyone noticing or commenting on its demise.

This short history illustrates perfectly the core drawback of tax credits in a modern state: the complexity of the modern tax system makes them invisible to the general public, thus also making it almost impossible to institutionalise them, and protect activities dependent upon them from chancellors in search of expenditure savings.

What of vouchers? The essential characteristic of a voucher is that it can be spent only on education, but the individual makes the choice of where to spend it and on what, in a more direct and immediate way than with 'virtual' systems, where money follows recruitment. The recipient institution receives money by cashing in the voucher. Most of the detailed voucher schemes that have made it into reality are at school level, and place quite considerable restraints on where vouchers can be 'spent' – in the sense that only certain types of school can receive them. Moreover children are full-time students for long periods, even though they can and do move schools during the course of what is now, typically, at least twelve years of full-time schooling. So a voucher recipient will receive a substantial sum per student, with relatively little attendant paperwork. 'Full' voucher systems remain rare, although virtual vouchers, in which students can choose their school, and funding is proportional to registered student numbers, are an increasingly common component of school funding systems.

One could, in principle, provide individuals with a number of 'mini-vouchers' to cash in (a bit like the money-off coupons beloved by food manufacturers, or like food stamps). But it is not obvious why, in an age of electronic banking and transfers, one would want to do anything so clumsy. This brings us to cash.

(C) Cash to the individual

A voucher is, in effect, a very specialised and unwieldy form of money. It can only be used for limited sorts of purchase; and, in the case of education vouchers, in very large denominations. The reason for providing vouchers rather than cash to people is to prevent recipients from using subsidies for the 'wrong' things: spending their food stamps on alcohol, or their education subsidies on holidays in the sun. Tax credits, too, have the advantage of limiting subsidies to the intended purchase: if audited, individuals must be able to prove that they have indeed spent the money on the 'right' thing.

We live today, however, in a world where financial transactions have been transformed. Huge proportions of purchases are made with cards, and leave permanent electronic records; transfers between accounts are swift and simple; and the nightmare of losing your credit rating means that the penalties for default on a loan – especially one where the government is involved – are serious.

If we want the provision of post-compulsory education and training to be highly sensitive to individual choice, then the best and most flexible way for this to be expressed is via individual, money-based payments. In the past, the costs of making and policing cash transfers to individuals specifically for education purchases appeared insuperably large. Today, this is, in my opinion, no longer the case. Across the world, student loan arrangements have been established which, in general, work well, and with very few technical problems. They have been overwhelmingly directed towards university students: but there is no reason, in principle, why both loans and direct subsidy payments cannot be made to a far wider range of students, for a far greater range of education and training.

In the UK, today, there is no uniform subsidy programme for individuals interested in obtaining post-compulsory education and training. On grounds of both efficiency and fairness, we should move to a uniform system based on two subsidy regimes. One, for long courses, would be based on the current English system for full-time undergraduates. Subsidies for intermittent adult education and training – 'short courses' – are more effectively channelled through some form of learning account. In both cases, a central-government-backed organisation should be responsible for making and collecting payments.

The way forward

(A) 'Long courses' and the higher education model

The way in which England and Wales currently fund universities and provide subsidies for 'home' undergraduates studying full-time is far from perfect, but nonetheless incorporates a number of excellent principles that can be generalised. The system is demonstrably working fairly well at present.[5] Any global 'league table' of top universities includes a fair number of UK institutions, and the country is second only to the USA in its appeal for overseas students. Participation rates did not fall, as was predicted, when the current fee-and-subsidy structure was introduced.[6] The approach can and should be generalised to all 'long' post-compulsory courses.

Defining a 'long course' from first principles is like deciding

5   Most of the discussion is about fee levels, not about the underlying structure.
6   The new fee structure increased the amount undergraduates pay, but reduced the amount they had to pay from their own resources at the time of enrolling and studying: fees are covered by income-contingent loans, repaid only when individuals start to earn.

at what point a number of stones becomes a heap. In practice, however, the education and training systems of the world offer a very similar set of alternatives, most of which fall naturally into a 'long' or 'short' category, reflecting the realities of life and labour markets. Long courses require a major commitment of time, and cannot normally be fitted in alongside a full-time paid job; and those completing them expect, at the end, to have acquired a major new set of skills and capabilities. They will typically require a least a year to complete: it is noteworthy that the only sorts of retraining and education courses for low-skilled adults that show significant economic gains are of two or more years' duration (see Chapter 3).

Long courses definitely include apprenticeships. These can work very much like higher education in funding terms; and, for adults (anyone over eighteen), they should do so.

The current subsidy regime for undergraduates builds on a contemporary consensus about the best way to address student risk aversion, and capital market failures (see Box 5 above).[7] Unlike with further education and adult training, governments do not get involved in 'picking winners', steering students towards these, and barring them from other degrees; but instead trust eighteen-year-olds (and their families) to make their own informed choices. Funding is 'mixed method', and combines individual subsidies with direct payments to institutions. The underlying subsidy structure for full-time undergraduates is as follows:[8]

---

7   See above, and Barr (2004), Barr and Crawford (2005).

8   In the discussion here, and in the general argument that subsidy patterns should be uniform across the post-compulsory sector, I refer only to teaching and teaching support, and not to research.

(i) Students pay fees, using money borrowed from a quasi-governmental provider of credit (Student Loans Company). The interest rate they incur, when repaying their loan, is subsidised; and loans are income-contingent, repaid only when earnings reach a given threshold. Students may also borrow additional funds for living expenses on a similar basis. This involves provision of a large amount of *cash to a provider of credit*.

(ii) Some students also receive direct cash grants or bursaries, provided they remain enrolled/studying; these are family-income-related and reflect the belief that students from poorer homes are more risk averse. These grants provide *cash directly to the individual* rather than via a provider of credit.

(iii) Fees cover only part of the cost of a course. The institution also receives funds for each student enrolled, directly from the state. This *'virtual voucher'* is paid annually: if students drop out, the payment for them also stops.

There are also streams of government funding which are institutional rather than dependent on student numbers, and restraints on what level of fee can be charged. And it is extremely difficult for successful institutions to expand their total number of subsidised home students: here there is an element of full-blown central planning which is strongly in need of reform.[9] But

---

9 At present, governments (through the funding councils) allocate a given number of home places to each institution: only these attract a 'virtual voucher' payment, and less successful institutions are protected because successful ones are not allowed to expand this part of their student body. Payments also differ according to the broad category of degree, with institutions receiving more money for their allocated science places than for their humanities places. Within these very broad categories, however, they are free to open, close, expand and contract particular degrees.

this is the basic underlying structure of subsidy.

The current undergraduate full-time model can and should be extended to part-time undergraduates, postgraduates, diploma students and apprentices, though it could, of course, in the short or long term, use different subsidy rates, payback periods, etc., outside the higher education sector.

(B) Back to the future: 'short courses' and Individual Learning Accounts

A distinctive and valuable aspect of post-compulsory education and training is that much of it is quite short-term and quite small-scale. People may undertake several aspects of study at once; and they often use quite different institutions for different study and training purposes.[10] In the non-subsidised, full-cost training market, it is noteworthy that a great deal of training is not formally accredited (which saves a large amount of expense and bureaucracy).

For frequent, short and geographically scattered education and training, a subsidy system that requires formal contracts and loans, tied to specific courses, could – indeed almost certainly would – become *administratively super-complex, with all the rigidities and expense this implies.* Coase, in his path-breaking analysis

---

10 A full-time two-year course is clearly 'long'. Italian for twenty weeks, one hour a week, is clearly 'short'. As always, there will be a blurred margin between the two categories. In practice, as already noted, most courses fall fairly clearly on one side of the divide or the other. And at the margin, which method someone uses to fund a course would probably depend as much on their own preferences for payment versus loan, how much was in their learning account, and what specific entitlement and subsidy rules a government introduces as to whether the course was more 'long' or more 'short'.

(1937), pointed out that institutions develop in situations where multiple small contracts would be extraordinarily expensive and time-consuming to operate. If we want to channel cash to individuals to subsidise their intermittent (and lifelong) learning, then we need some sort of institution that circumvents the need for repeated new contracts and invoices.

The method recommended here is the learning account. These allow individuals to pay cash into their accounts in varying amounts, and receive corresponding benefits in the form of matched funding, interest subsidies or periodic payments from the government. Such accounts allow for a variety of approaches to, and levels of, subsidy. Individuals can then use their accounts to help pay for whatever they want to learn, in whatever form they want to learn, whenever they want.

As noted earlier, the near-universality of IT, including its impact on financial transactions, has genuinely changed the environment in and through which individual demand can be expressed. The vast majority of adults – including older adults – have IT access and an even larger proportion of the population uses bank or modern post office accounts. We have surely now reached a point where we can use market-type mechanisms across the post-compulsory subsidised sector, using direct payments to and by individuals to increase its responsiveness to their preferences.

Moreover, an excellent model already exists for an agency to run such Individual Learning Accounts, in the form of the Charities Aid Foundation. This already operates accounts that are, structurally, exactly like ILAs. Individuals – many thousands of them – pay funds in and the Foundation tops them up with the tax relief allowed on charitable contributions by government:

when the level of relief changes, so does the top-up. The organisation is extremely efficient, and operates a system of payments only to approved providers which to date has been immune from fraud. The contrasting recent histories of the UK's Student Loans Company and of the US multiply-sourced student finance system also argue strongly in favour of a single, regulated lender and banker.[11] High levels of risk and uncertainty for private lenders, plus the ease and temptation of creating (illegal) partnerships between lenders and institutions, have produced both inefficiencies and scandals in the US higher education loan market.

Individual Learning Accounts have been advocated for some decades, but there is rather little experience on which to draw, here or abroad.[12] Moreover, they currently have a bad reputation in Whitehall because of New Labour's ill-fated programme of the early 2000s. The idea tends to evoke an automatic response along the lines of: 'But they don't work. There was all that fraud. It's just not practical.'

That response is quite wrong. First, the programme was not, as the Commons Select Committee later observed, in any real sense an ILA programme at all (House of Commons Education and Skills Committee, 2002). It was actually a rather complex and bureaucratic form of (low-value) voucher. It channelled funds to approved providers; to obtain these funds, learners had to be signed up and registered with a single, specified college or trainer on an individual basis, after which the institution could apply

---

11   One recurrent problem in the USA is that competing loan companies try to persuade/pay college staff to direct students towards one particular company (without making their links to the company public). See, for example, various stories carried by the *Higher Education Chronicle*: http://chronicle.com

12   The government is currently piloting a new form of account, but it appears to be no more a genuine ILA than was its predecessor.

for and receive money. It also covered only a highly limited set of options; the funds could not be used in a general way at all.

Second, the reason it failed had everything to do with a classic governmental determination to rush an IT system into use, without giving adequate development time, and with multiple design changes during the development phase. This made some fraud possible, although the House of Commons' exhaustive inquiry indicates that the amount of fraud was, in fact, quite small. (The whole programme was closed down as soon as it became clear that the IT system used for registration was open to abuse.)

That the initiative was poorly conceived, poorly executed, highly bureaucratic, and generated a (rather small) amount of fraud does not in any way undermine the basic arguments for such accounts. On the contrary, what the ILA experiment actually did was indicate that large numbers of people are very interested indeed in undertaking further, short-term subsidised learning. In other words, *the mechanism works*.

Post-compulsory, and especially further and adult, education are characterised by complexity of demand – people want to study at different times, with different intensity, sometimes for short-term employment reasons, sometimes for longer-term or more developmental ones, sometimes to top up existing skills, sometimes to learn totally new ones. As I have argued elsewhere, the sector's current organisation reflects governmental disdain for the non-graduate, non-professional segments of society, who are not trusted to make their own decisions (Wolf, 2007a). The best way to ensure that individuals have access to the education and training they want and from which they can benefit is by putting the choice in their hands and providing subsidies that affect the prices they pay. Learning accounts provide a flexible, and entirely practicable, method of achieving this, and are especially well suited to short and intermittent purchases.

Paying for it all: changing the way government spends money

Overall, the reforms will be affordable for the simple reason that there is a great deal of wasted 'fat' in the current system. At the very least, for a given level of government spending, a much more efficient use of funds will be achieved if the proposed funding reforms are implemented. A recurrent thread in this monograph has been the value of using higher education as a comparator – a system that is clearer, more efficient, far more autonomous and relatively free of government interference, and which really does achieve the 'world class' status of which our politicians talk so endlessly. One of the most telling differences between the 'advanced' (HE) and 'non-advanced' (FE and training) systems is the difference in the amount, and proportion, of expenditure allocated to central administration, and to the piling up of over-lapping governmental and quasi-governmental bodies. It is worth reiterating that *as a proportion of expenditure disbursed, the Learning and Skills Council spends ten times as much as HEFCE* – and not because it is intrinsically wasteful or inefficient but because of the tasks it is set by interventionist ministers.

Table 7 summarises current government spending on this sector. Most of the spending on non-university activities is channelled through the Learning and Skills Council, soon to be replaced by three separate new quangos. The other main spending headings mostly relate to payments to quangos. Of the £452 million spent by DIUS on activities other than those currently administered by the LSC, at least half (£226 million) could be cut tomorrow, including the funding to RDAs and the UK Commission/SSC network.

Within the LSC budget, a growing proportion – scheduled to exceed £1 billion in 2008/09 – is directed to the Train to Gain programme, which, it was argued above, is unjustifiable in principle, and failing to produce any useful results. 'Adult skills reform' and 'quality reform' consist of a considerable number of small programmes, most of which would be entirely unnecessary under a genuinely demand-driven regime (e.g. Skills for Life marketing, Qualifications and Credit Framework). Comparisons with HE suggest that at least three-quarters of the LSC's own heavy administrative costs (some £150 million out of £200 million) are a direct result of current misconceived and micromanaged programmes.

In addition, much of the expenditure on current apprenticeships is a waste of money. And so is a very high proportion of what is currently spent within other categories: on NVQs with zero returns, internal FE administrative costs, etc. A conservative estimate is that £2 *billion a year could be diverted, immediately, to far more productive and valuable use, with nothing valuable lost in the process.*

Table 7 also highlights the inequities in student support that were outlined earlier (Table 5). £1.2 billion a year is currently being spent on student maintenance grants to overwhelmingly young full-time students – 12 per cent of the HE budget, and a quarter of the entire FE and skills budget. FE, by comparison, with its far less advantaged student body, receives £167 million. The huge expenditures on university students are a result of a

Table 7 **Expenditure on post-compulsory education and training, 2008/09**

(A) Summary by sector	£ millions
Higher education	9,763
Student support grants	(1,198)
Further education and skills	4,852
Learning and Skills Council	(4,440)
Regional Development Agencies	(42)
UK Commission on Skills/Sector Skills Councils	(83)
'FE improvement'	(154)
Other miscellaneous	(132)
(B) Learning and Skills Council expenditure, 2008/09	
Total (FE and skills, + 16–18-yr-olds, inc. school sixth forms)	12,072
Selected programmes and costs:	
19+ further education	1,499
Adult safeguarded learning (adult and community)	214
Train to Gain	876
Adult skills reform	80
Quality reform	83
Adult (19+ apprenticeships)	347
Administration costs	200
Student support	167

Sources: DIUS Annual Report, 2008/09; LSC Annual Report and Accounts, 2008/09

politically motivated decision, taken at the very start of the Brown premiership, to increase enormously the number of university students receiving grants (as opposed to loans). The cost of this was initially underestimated by a very wide margin, and the FE budget raided to cover the shortfall.

Simply merging the two support budgets and allocating them equally across the whole student population would be an enormous step forward to a fairer and more efficient system. It also requires political will: removing entitlements is a lot harder than bestowing them. But even middle-class students are not that vital or powerful an interest group, and they turn over fast!

Keeping spending within bounds

There are large amounts of money which can be redirected, even under conditions of acute financial stringency. Whatever holds back reform, it will not, one must conclude, be the impossibility of funding it. Nonetheless, the cost of reform, and more specifically the long-term costs of my recommended structure, do matter.

At present we have a system in which, outside the universities, the government decides precisely how much education and training in total, and what sort of education and training in detail, will be purchased; pays for it; and leaves it to the providers to find people who are willing to fill the places created. This ought to give it total control of costs, although, as we have seen, government departments have, even so, managed to lose all control of spending on several recent occasions.

At university level, there is also a decision about how many places in total will be funded, although far less control of detail. Currently, this country, like many others, operates strict cash limits at university level by the simple expedient of fixing the total number of places it will fund in the heavily subsidised part of the system.[13] Although students pay a significant part of the cost, the state also provides a great deal of money directly (as well as through loan subsidies to the student), most particularly for undergraduate education. By fixing the number of undergraduate

---

13 In the other parts of higher education, there is no such control; a market operates, with universities offering courses and setting fees freely.

places it will 'match fund' in this way, it controls expenditures quite precisely. If more people want to take an undergraduate degree than there are funded places in a given year, then that is just their misfortune.

Treasury officials remember clearly that, on the one occasion in the 1990s when they allowed, and funded, universities to expand undergraduate places relatively freely, in response to any increase in qualified applicants, demand and spending soared. And, as described above, the one small experiment with Individual Learning Accounts indicated that there was a large untapped demand for short subsidised courses. Both these examples involved very high subsidy rates – 100 per cent of fees in the case of undergraduate courses at the time (fees having been reintroduced for English universities only in the late 1990s) and 80 per cent on many of the courses covered under the ILA scheme. But people forecasted big drops in university attendance when higher fees were introduced: in fact no such drop occurred, in line with Australian and New Zealand experience.

So there could indeed be serious difficulties if the system was demand-led with an open-ended commitment to provide matched funding and subsidies. Few FE courses are likely to cost anything like as much as a degree, but big changes in total (subsidised) demand, and, therefore, government expenditure are possible. Clearly people are very willing to incur debts for a product they value.[14] A shift to a genuinely demand-led system, rather than

14 One can confidently predict a higher volume of spending in total, with a much increased proportion from private individuals, especially in FE. As noted earlier, it is extraordinary that at present English FE colleges, in contrast to universities, raise only about 7 per cent of their income from fees (Fletcher and Perry, 2008; Corney and Fletcher, 2007). This reflects a system in which some people are offered 100 per cent subsidies, while others are offered no subsidy at all.

the current centrally planned one, might create a big increase in demand – especially if quality improves.[15]

Governments do need to introduce cash limits for activities for both the 'short course' and the 'long course' part of the sector. Of the two, the former is actually easier to control, because of the nature of the learning accounts mechanism.

One critical and important feature of accounts is that they separate the paying out of subsidies by government – into people's learning accounts – from the purchases individuals make. The government can simply cash-limit the amount of subsidy it pays into individuals' learning accounts over a given time period: each person is entitled to a set amount in total. This could be a lump sum; or, if contributions to ILAs were on a matching basis, there would simply have to be a cap on the total extent of the matching. There could also be a subsidised credit mechanism, for some or all savers, reducing interest on any account overdraft or on loans paid into the account. This approach has the enormous benefit of flexibility, which is especially suited to the bulk of adult education and training.

Deposits would, quite naturally, tend be spread over a period well in advance of enrolment (and spending); and depositors could, and almost inevitably would, expect and experience some delay between making deposits and receiving their matching payment (as happens with charity accounts). Such a system has the additional advantage, as opposed to loans, that costs to government are immediate and up-front.

All of this enables a government (via a competent subsidiary) to monitor payments effectively. If payments are on track to be

---

15   Messer and Wolter (2009) show that demand is higher when adults have vouchers they can use freely than when they simply have access to well-funded public institutions.

greater than expected in a given time period, it can change the subsidy rates – but this will happen in advance of future deposits, so that account holders know what to expect. The decision of what to spend, when and with which institutions, meanwhile, rests with the individual.

For the large sums of money needed for long and substantial courses, loans with income-contingent repayments are, as discussed earlier, the best approach.[16] Additional funding for these can come from those current activities which, I have suggested, could be terminated tomorrow.

Limits on how much people can borrow should be set in cash terms (over a lifetime) rather than in terms of detailed entitlements to particular types of course or qualification. This would eradicate the current unjustified distinction between full-time undergraduate and all other forms of study. Lifetime credit limits do not, however, control expenditure in a given year, something that the Treasury would naturally want to ensure.

Currently in higher education, the total volume of spending is controlled by a cap on 'home' university places, which carry subsidies. This may or may not be the best way to control higher education spending; in any case it is possible only because university degrees are very standardised in length and structure.[17] It would

---

16 The high up-front cost of loans is a major problem for governments wishing to expand provision, although this is partly an artefact of the way government spending is defined and treated in the accounts. An additional problem with the current system in England is the high cost of interest subsidies, which continue over a very long period; but there is no reason, in fact, why interest rates should be as heavily subsidised as they are at present.

17 Whether or not this is desirable, it is not going to change in the future: on the contrary. Intergovernmental agreements such as the Bologna agreement, plus the demands of an increasingly international clientele, are creating ever greater standardisation of structure (as opposed to content) across the world.

be wholly inappropriate in the further education sector, where there is such diversity in the nature of provision, to have an overall 'cap' on places. Total spending can instead be kept in bounds in a number of ways: by varying the total *amount* of subsidy that is available for each individual, by capping numbers of loans on a quarterly or annual basis, and by varying other grants made available to further education institutions and payments to employers who accept apprentices.

Conclusion

The idea that one can plan for anything as complex as the modern labour market would be laughable if it were not that we are wasting vast sums of money in the attempt to do so. Conversely, recent experience – with the ILAs, but also with the unregulated, postgraduate and 'overseas' elements of higher education – demonstrates that an education and training market develops very easily. It provides highly varied and popular programmes when the mechanism for relating demand and supply exists. Instead of forcing institutions to spend their time and energy negotiating with, and being instructed as well as funded by, public sector paymasters, we can and should free them to respond directly to learners' demands. In particular, we should divert the large sums of money currently wasted by our post-compulsory education and training system to developing an equitable system of student support and loans across the whole of nineteen-plus education, and a national system of learning accounts which places demand genuinely, and productively, in the hands of individual learners.

REFERENCES

Aaronovitch, D. (2009), 'I'll show you mine if you show me yours', *The Times*, 29 May 2009.

Abramovsky, L. (2006), 'Lots of initiatives, but still a productivity gap', *The Edge*, 21, Swindon: Economic and Social Research Council.

Abramovsky, L. et al. (2005), 'The impact of the employer training pilots on the take-up of training among employers and employees', Research Report 694, London: Institute for Fiscal Studies.

Acemoglu, D. and J.-S. Pischke (1999), 'Beyond Becker: training in imperfect labor markets', *Economic Journal*, 109: 112–42.

Aldridge, F. and A. Tuckett (2008), *Counting the Cost: The NIACE Survey of Adult Participation in Learning*, Leicester: NIACE.

Asplund, R. (2004), *The Provision and Effects of Company Training*, DP 907, Helsinki: ETLA (Research Institute of the Finnish Economy).

Bach, S. (2009), 'Public sector employment relations; the challenge of modernisation', in T. Colling and M. Terry, *Industrial Relations*, 3rd edn, London: Wiley.

Bailey, B. (2001), 'Further education', in R. Aldrich, *A Century of Education*, London: Routledge Falmer.

Barr, N. (2004), 'Higher education funding', *Oxford Review of Economic Policy*, 20(2): 264–83.

Barr, N. and I. Crawford (2005), *Financing Higher Education. Lessons from the UK*, London: Routledge.

Becker, G. S. (1993 [1964]), *Human Capital: A Theoretical and Empirical Analysis with Special Reference to Education*, 3rd edn, Chicago, IL: Chicago University Press.

Black, S. E., L. Lynch and L. Krivelyova (2003), *How Workers Fare When Employers Innovate*, WP 9569, Cambridge, MA: NBER.

Blunkett, D. (2001), 'Education into employability: the role of the DfEE in the economy', Speech delivered at the Institute of Economic Affairs, London, 24 January, London: Department for Education and Employment.

Brown, P. and A. Hesketh (2004), *The Mismanagement of Talent: Employability and Jobs in the Knowledge Economy*, Oxford: Oxford University Press.

CEREQ (2008), *Les Chemins de la formation vers l'emploi*, Marseilles: CEREQ.

Coase, R. (1937), 'The nature of the firm', *Economica*, 4(16): 386–405.

Collins, R. (1990), 'Changing conceptions in the sociology of the professions', in R. Torstendahl and M. Burrage (eds), *The Formation of Professions: Knowledge, State and Strategy*, London: Sage.

Corney, M. (2007), *Still Waiting for Big Ideas on Adult Skills*, Reading: CfBT Education Trust.

Corney, M. and M. Fletcher (2007), *Adult Skills and Higher Education: Separation or Union?*, Reading: CfBT Education Trust.

Davies, P., J. Mangan and A. Hughes (2009), 'Participation, financial support and the marginal student', *Higher Education*, 58(2): 175–91.

Dearden, L., L. McGranahan and B. Sianesi (2004), *An In-Depth Analysis of the Returns to National Vocational Qualifications Obtained at Level 2*, Centre for the Economics of Education Discussion Paper 46, London: LSE.

Delorenzi, S. (2007), *Learning for Life: A new framework for adult skills*, London: IPPR.

DfES (Department for Education and Skills) (2001), *Skills for Life: The national strategy for improving adult literacy and numeracy skills*, London: DfES.

Dickerson, A. (2008), *The Distribution and Returns to Qualifications in the Four Countries of the UK*, Research Report 21A, Wath-upon-Dearne: Sector Skills Development Agency.

Dolton, P. J., G. H. Makepeace and J. G. Treble (1994), 'The wage effect of YTS', *Scottish Journal of Political Economy*, 41: 444–54.

Dolton, P. J., G. H. Makepeace and B. M. Gannon (2001), 'The earnings and employment effects of young people's vocational training in Britain', *The Manchester School*, 69(4): 387–417.

Encyclopedia of Higher Education (1992), Oxford: Pergamon.

Fazackerley, A. and J. Chant (2008), *The Hard Truth about 'Soft' Subjects*, London: Policy Exchange.

Fazackerley, A., C. Callender, J. Chant and D. Wilkinson (2009), *Educating Rita? A model to address inadequate state support for part-time students*, London: Policy Exchange.

Finegold, D. and D. Soskice (1988), 'The failure of training in Britain: analysis and prescription', *Oxford Review of Economic Policy*, 4: 21–53.

Fletcher, M. and A. Perry (2008), *By Accident or Design: Is our system of post-16 provision fit for purpose?*, Reading: CfBT Education Trust.

Foster, A. (2005), *Realising the Future: A review of the future role of further education colleges*, London: DfES.

Foster, A. (2009), *A Review of the Capital Programme in Further Education*, London: Department of Innovation, Universities and Skills (DIUS).

Friedman, M. (1955), 'The role of government in education', in R. A. Solo (ed.), *Economics and the Public Interest*, New Brunswick, NJ: Rutgers University Press.

Fuller, A. and L. Unwin (2003), 'Creating a "Modern Apprenticeship": a critique of the UK's multi-sector, social inclusion approach', *Journal of Education and Work*, 16(1): 5–25.

Fuller, A. and L. Unwin (2008), *Towards Expansive Apprenticeships*, Teaching and Learning Research Programme: A Commentary, Swindon: ESRC Teaching and Learning Research Programme.

Glennester, H., Merrett, S. and Wilson, G. (1968), 'A graduate tax', *Higher Education Review*, 1.1, 26–38.

Graham, G. (2005), *The Institution of Intellectual Values: Realism and Idealism in Higher Education*, London: Academic.

Green, F., M. Hoskins and S. Montgomery (1996), 'The effects of company training, further education and the Youth Training Scheme on the earnings of young employees', *Oxford Bulletin of Economics and Statistics*, 58: 469–88.

Griffith, R. (2007), 'Technology, productivity and public policy', *Fiscal Studies*, 28(3): 273–91.

Haldenby, A., H. Rainbow, L. Thraves and E. Triss (2008), *The Mobile Economy*, London: Reform.

Heckman, J., R. LaLonde and J. Smith (1999), 'The economics and econometrics of active labor market programs', in O. Ashenfelter and D. Card (eds), *Handbook of Labor Economics*, vol. 3, Amsterdam: North-Holland, pp. 1865–2097.

House of Commons Education and Skills Committee (2002), *Individual Learning Accounts: Third report of session 2001–2*, London: The Stationery Office.

House of Commons Education and Skills Committee (2007), *Post-16 Skills: Ninth report of session 2006–7*, London: The Stationery Office.

House of Commons Innovation, Universities, Science and Skills Committee (2009), *Spend, Spend, Spend? The mismanagement of the Learning and Skills Council's capital programme in further education colleges: seventh report of session 2008–9*, London: The Stationery Office.

House of Lords Economic Affairs Committee (2007), *Apprenticeship: Fifth report of the 2006–7 session*, London: House of Lords.

Hutchins, R. M. (1953), *The University of Utopia: Charles R. Walgreen Foundation Lectures*, Chicago, IL: University of Chicago Press.

Jenkins, A. and A. Wolf (2002), 'Why do employers use selection tests? Evidence from British workplaces', CEE Discussion Paper no. 27, London: Centre for the Economics of Education, LSE.

Jenkins, A. and A. Wolf (2005), 'Employers' selection decisions: the role of qualifications and tests', in S. Machin and A. Vignoles (eds), *What's the Good of Education? The Economics of Education in the UK*, Princeton, NJ: Princeton University Press.

Jenkins, A., A. Vignoles, A. Wolf and F. Galindo-Rueda (2004), 'The determinants and labour market effects of lifelong learning', *Applied Economics*, 35: 1711–21.

Jenkins, A., C. Greenwood and A. Vignoles (2007), 'The returns to qualifications in England: updating the evidence base on Level 2 and Level 3 vocational qualifications', Working Paper 47, London: Centre for the Economics of Education, LSE.

Jessup, G. (1991), *Outcomes: NVQs and the Emerging Model of Education and Training*, London: Falmer.

Johansen, L. H. (2000), *Transferable Training and the Collective Action Problem for Employers*, Repport 335, Oslo: Forskningsstiftelsen Fafo.

Kay, J. (2003), *The Truth about Markets*, London: Penguin Press.

Keep, E., K. Mayhew and J. Payne (2006), 'From skills revolution to productivity miracle – not as easy as it sounds?', *Oxford Review of Economic Policy*, 22(4): 539–59.

Layard, R., K. Mayhew and G. Owen (eds) (1994), *Britain's Training Deficit*, Aldershot: Avebury Press.

Lechner, M., R. Miquel and C. Wunch (2004), *Long-run Effects of Public Sector Sponsored Training in West Germany*, DP 1443, Bonn: IZA.

Leitch, S. (2006), *Prosperity for All in the Global Economy – World Class Skills: Final Report* (Leitch Review of Skills), London: The Stationery Office for HM Treasury.

Levy, F. and R. Murnane (2004), *The New Division of Labor: How Computers Are Changing the Way We Work*, Princeton, NJ: Princeton University Press.

Lewis, P. A. and P. Ryan (2009a), 'External inspection and the role of employers in the apprenticeship programme in England's training market', *Empirical Research in Vocational Education and Training*, 1: 44–68.

Lewis, P. A. and P. Ryan (2009b), 'The role of external inspection in the public services: the case of the UK training market', *Public Administration*. (Online, 'Early View'.)

Linford, N. (2008), *The Hands-on Guide to Post-16 Funding*, London: Edexcel.

Machin, S., S. McIntosh, A. Vignoles and T. Viitanen (2001), *Basic Skills, Soft Skills and Labour Market Outcomes: Secondary analysis of the National Child Development Study (RR250)*, London: DfEE.

Mansell, W. (2007), *Education by Numbers: The Tyranny of Testing*, London: Politico's.

McIntosh, S. (2004), 'The impact of vocational qualifications on the labour market outcomes of low-achieving school-leavers', Discussion Paper no. 641, London: Centre for Economic Performance, LSE.

Messer, D. and S. Wolter (2009), *Money Matters: Evidence from a Large-scale Randomized Field Experiment with Vouchers for Adult Training*, DP 4017 Bonn: IZA.

Moser, C./DfEE (Department for Education and Employment) (1999), *Improving Literacy and Numeracy: A fresh start*, Report of the working group chaired by Sir Claus Moser, London: DfEE.

MSC (Manpower Services Commission) (1981), *A New Training Initiative: A Consultation Document*, Sheffield: MSC.

Myddelton, D. R. (2007), *They Meant Well: Government Project Disasters*, London: IEA.

Oakley, K. and D. O'Leary (2008), *The Skills Paradox: Confronting Inequality in Adult Learning*, London: Demos.

OECD (2008), *Education at a Glance: OECD Indicators*, Paris: OECD.

PIU (Performance and Innovation Unit) (2001), *In Demand: Adult skills in the 21st century*, London: PIU.

Pritchett, L. (2001), 'Where has all the education gone?', *World Bank Economic Review*, 15(3): 367–91.

Richardson, K. and G. van den Berg (2006), 'Swedish labour market training and the duration of unemployment', Discussion Paper 2314, Bonn: IZA.

Rose, J. (2002), *The Intellectual Life of the British Working Classes*, New Haven, CT: Yale Nota Bene.

Ryan, P. (2004), 'Apprentice strikes in the twentieth century UK engineering and shipbuilding industries', *Historical Studies in Industrial Relations*, 18: 1–63.

Ryan, P. and L. Unwin (2001), 'Apprenticeship in the British training market', *National Institute Economic Review*, 178: 70–85.

Ryan, P., H. Gospel and P. A. Lewis (2007), 'Large employers and apprenticeship training in the UK', *British Journal of Industrial Relations*, 45: 127–53.

Schuller, T. and Watson, D. (2009), *Learning Through Life: Inquiry into the Future for Lifelong Learning*, Leicester: NIACE.

Scottish Executive (2004), *Review of Funding of Learners*, Edinburgh: Scottish Executive.

Shackleton, J. R. (1992), *Training Too Much? A Sceptical Look at the Economics of Skill Provision in the UK*, Hobart Paper 118, London: IEA.

Siegrist, M., H. Gutscher and T. Earle (2005), 'Perception of risk: the influence of general trust and general confidence', *Journal of Risk Research*, 5(2): 145–56.

Stanton, G. (1996), *Output-related Funding and the Quality of Education and Training*, London: Institute of Education.

Stanton, G. (2008), *Learning Matters. Making the 14–19 reforms work for learners*, Reading: CfBT Education Trust.

Sutton Trust (2009), *Access to the Professions*, London: Sutton Trust.

Tooley, J. (2009), *The Beautiful Tree: A Personal Journey into How the World's Poorest People Are Educating Themselves*, Washington, DC: Cato Institute.

Vasager, J. and R. Smithers (2003), 'Will Charles Clarke have his place in history?', *Guardian*, 10 May.

Vignoles, A. and A. de Coulon (2008), 'An analysis of the benefit of NVQ2 qualifications acquired at ages 26–34', CEE DP106, London: Centre for the Economics of Education, LSE.

Wells, A. (2008), 'Going to the football does me good, but it isn't free', *Guardian Education*, 26 June.

Whitfield, K. and C. Bourlakis (1991), 'An empirical analysis of YTS, employment and earning', *Journal of Economic Studies*, 18(1): 42–56.

Wilensky, H. L. (1964), 'The professionalization of everyone?', *American Journal of Sociology*, 70(2): 137–58.

Wolf, A. (1997), 'Growth stocks and lemons: diplomas in the English market-place 1976–1996', *Assessment in Education*, 4(1): 33–49.

Wolf, A. (2001), 'Qualifications and assessment', in R. Aldrich (ed.), *A Century of Education*, London: Routledge Falmer, pp. 206–27.

Wolf, A. (2002), *Does Education Matter? Myths about Education and Economic Growth*, London: Penguin.

Wolf, A. (2004), 'Education and economic performance: simplistic theories and the policy consequences', *Oxford Review of Economic Policy*, 20(2): 315–33.

Wolf, A. (2007a) 'Why do governments treat further education students like children?', in D. Kehoe (ed.), *Practice Makes Perfect: The Importance of Practical Learning*, London: Social Market Foundation.

Wolf, A. (2007b) 'Round and round the houses: the Leitch Review of Skills', *Local Economy*, 22(3): 111–17.

Wolf, A. (2008), *Diminished Returns. How Raising the Leaving Age to 18 Will Harm Young People and the Economy*, London: Policy Exchange.

Wolf, A., A. Jenkins and A. Vignoles (2006), 'Certifying the workforce: economic imperative or failed social policy?', *Journal of Education Policy*, 21(5): 535–66.

Wolf, A., K. Evans, L. Aspin, E. Waite and A. Jenkins (2009), *Final Report to the ESRC on Project RES-139–25–0120: 'Enhancing "Skills for Life": adult basic skills and workplace learning'*, Swindon: ESRC.

Wolf, A., A. Aspin, E. Waite and A. Ananiadou (forthcoming), 'Lessons from the rise and fall of workplace basic skills programmes', *Oxford Review of Education*.

ABOUT THE IEA

The Institute is a research and educational charity (No. CC 235 351), limited by guarantee. Its mission is to improve understanding of the fundamental institutions of a free society by analysing and expounding the role of markets in solving economic and social problems.

The IEA achieves its mission by:

- a high-quality publishing programme
- conferences, seminars, lectures and other events
- outreach to school and college students
- brokering media introductions and appearances

The IEA, which was established in 1955 by the late Sir Antony Fisher, is an educational charity, not a political organisation. It is independent of any political party or group and does not carry on activities intended to affect support for any political party or candidate in any election or referendum, or at any other time. It is financed by sales of publications, conference fees and voluntary donations.

In addition to its main series of publications the IEA also publishes a quarterly journal, *Economic Affairs*.

The IEA is aided in its work by a distinguished international Academic Advisory Council and an eminent panel of Honorary Fellows. Together with other academics, they review prospective IEA publications, their comments being passed on anonymously to authors. All IEA papers are therefore subject to the same rigorous independent refereeing process as used by leading academic journals.

IEA publications enjoy widespread classroom use and course adoptions in schools and universities. They are also sold throughout the world and often translated/reprinted.

Since 1974 the IEA has helped to create a worldwide network of 100 similar institutions in over 70 countries. They are all independent but share the IEA's mission.

Views expressed in the IEA's publications are those of the authors, not those of the Institute (which has no corporate view), its Managing Trustees, Academic Advisory Council members or senior staff.

Members of the Institute's Academic Advisory Council, Honorary Fellows, Trustees and Staff are listed on the following page.

The Institute gratefully acknowledges financial support for its publications programme and other work from a generous benefaction by the late Alec and Beryl Warren.

The Institute of Economic Affairs
2 Lord North Street, Westminster, London SW1P 3LB
Tel: 020 7799 8900
Fax: 020 7799 2137
Email: iea@iea.org.uk
Internet: iea.org.uk

181

Other papers recently published by the IEA include:

A Market in Airport Slots
Keith Boyfield (editor), David Starkie, Tom Bass & Barry Humphreys
Readings 56; ISBN 0 255 36505 5; £10.00

Money, Inflation and the Constitutional Position of the Central Bank
Milton Friedman & Charles A. E. Goodhart
Readings 57; ISBN 0 255 36538 1; £10.00

railway.com
Parallels between the Early British Railways and the ICT Revolution
Robert C. B. Miller
Research Monograph 57; ISBN 0 255 36534 9; £12.50

The Regulation of Financial Markets
Edited by Philip Booth & David Currie
Readings 58; ISBN 0 255 36551 9; £12.50

Climate Alarmism Reconsidered
Robert L. Bradley Jr
Hobart Paper 146; ISBN 0 255 36541 1; £12.50

Government Failure: E. G. West on Education
Edited by James Tooley & James Stanfield
Occasional Paper 130; ISBN 0 255 36552 7; £12.50

Corporate Governance: Accountability in the Marketplace
Elaine Sternberg
Second edition
Hobart Paper 147; ISBN 0 255 36542 X; £12.50

The Land Use Planning System
Evaluating Options for Reform
John Corkindale
Hobart Paper 148; ISBN 0 255 36550 0; £10.00

Economy and Virtue
Essays on the Theme of Markets and Morality
Edited by Dennis O'Keeffe
Readings 59; ISBN 0 255 36504 7; £12.50

Free Markets Under Siege
Cartels, Politics and Social Welfare
Richard A. Epstein
Occasional Paper 132; ISBN 0 255 36553 5; £10.00

Unshackling Accountants
D. R. Myddelton
Hobart Paper 149; ISBN 0 255 36559 4; £12.50

The Euro as Politics
Pedro Schwartz
Research Monograph 58; ISBN 0 255 36535 7; £12.50

Pricing Our Roads
Vision and Reality
Stephen Glaister & Daniel J. Graham
Research Monograph 59; ISBN 0 255 36562 4; £10.00

The Role of Business in the Modern World
Progress, Pressures, and Prospects for the Market Economy
David Henderson
Hobart Paper 150; ISBN 0 255 36548 9; £12.50

Public Service Broadcasting Without the BBC?
Alan Peacock
Occasional Paper 133; ISBN 0 255 36565 9; £10.00

The ECB and the Euro: the First Five Years
Otmar Issing
Occasional Paper 134; ISBN 0 255 36555 1; £10.00

Towards a Liberal Utopia?
Edited by Philip Booth
Hobart Paperback 32; ISBN 0 255 36563 2; £15.00

The Way Out of the Pensions Quagmire
Philip Booth & Deborah Cooper
Research Monograph 60; ISBN 0 255 36517 9; £12.50

Black Wednesday
A Re-examination of Britain's Experience in the Exchange Rate Mechanism
Alan Budd
Occasional Paper 135; ISBN 0 255 36566 7; £7.50

Crime: Economic Incentives and Social Networks
Paul Ormerod
Hobart Paper 151; ISBN 0 255 36554 3; £10.00

The Road to Serfdom *with* **The Intellectuals and Socialism**
Friedrich A. Hayek
Occasional Paper 136; ISBN 0 255 36576 4; £10.00

Money and Asset Prices in Boom and Bust
Tim Congdon
Hobart Paper 152; ISBN 0 255 36570 5; £10.00

The Dangers of Bus Re-regulation
and Other Perspectives on Markets in Transport
John Hibbs et al.
Occasional Paper 137; ISBN 0 255 36572 1; £10.00

The New Rural Economy
Change, Dynamism and Government Policy
Berkeley Hill et al.
Occasional Paper 138; ISBN 0 255 36546 2; £15.00

The Benefits of Tax Competition
Richard Teather
Hobart Paper 153; ISBN 0 255 36569 1; £12.50

Wheels of Fortune
Self-funding Infrastructure and the Free Market Case for a Land Tax
Fred Harrison
Hobart Paper 154; ISBN 0 255 36589 6; £12.50

Were 364 Economists All Wrong?
Edited by Philip Booth
Readings 60; ISBN 978 0 255 36588 8; £10.00

Europe After the 'No' Votes
Mapping a New Economic Path
Patrick A. Messerlin
Occasional Paper 139; ISBN 978 0 255 36580 2; £10.00

The Railways, the Market and the Government
John Hibbs et al.
Readings 61; ISBN 978 0 255 36567 3; £12.50

Corruption: The World's Big C
Cases, Causes, Consequences, Cures
Ian Senior
Research Monograph 61; ISBN 978 0 255 36571 0; £12.50

Choice and the End of Social Housing
Peter King
Hobart Paper 155; ISBN 978 0 255 36568 0; £10.00

Sir Humphrey's Legacy
Facing Up to the Cost of Public Sector Pensions
Neil Record
Hobart Paper 156; ISBN 978 0 255 36578 9; £10.00

The Economics of Law
Cento Veljanovski
Second edition
Hobart Paper 157; ISBN 978 0 255 36561 1; £12.50

Living with Leviathan
Public Spending, Taxes and Economic Performance
David B. Smith
Hobart Paper 158; ISBN 978 0 255 36579 6; £12.50

The Vote Motive
Gordon Tullock
New edition
Hobart Paperback 33; ISBN 978 0 255 36577 2; £10.00

Waging the War of Ideas
John Blundell
Third edition
Occasional Paper 131; ISBN 978 0 255 36606 9; £12.50

The War Between the State and the Family
How Government Divides and Impoverishes
Patricia Morgan
Hobart Paper 159; ISBN 978 0 255 36596 3; £10.00

Capitalism – A Condensed Version
Arthur Seldon
Occasional Paper 140; ISBN 978 0 255 36598 7; £7.50

Catholic Social Teaching and the Market Economy
Edited by Philip Booth
Hobart Paperback 34; ISBN 978 0 255 36581 9; £15.00

Adam Smith – A Primer
Eamonn Butler
Occasional Paper 141; ISBN 978 0 255 36608 3; £7.50

Happiness, Economics and Public Policy
Helen Johns & Paul Ormerod
Research Monograph 62; ISBN 978 0 255 36600 7; £10.00

They Meant Well
Government Project Disasters
D. R. Myddelton
Hobart Paper 160; ISBN 978 0 255 36601 4; £12.50

Rescuing Social Capital from Social Democracy
John Meadowcroft & Mark Pennington
Hobart Paper 161; ISBN 978 0 255 36592 5; £10.00

Paths to Property
Approaches to Institutional Change in International Development
Karol Boudreaux & Paul Dragos Aligica
Hobart Paper 162; ISBN 978 0 255 36582 6; £10.00

Prohibitions
Edited by John Meadowcroft
Hobart Paperback 35; ISBN 978 0 255 36585 7; £15.00

Trade Policy, New Century
The WTO, FTAs and Asia Rising
Razeen Sally
Hobart Paper 163; ISBN 978 0 255 36544 4; £12.50

Sixty Years On – Who Cares for the NHS?
Helen Evans
Research Monograph 63; ISBN 978 0 255 36611 3; £10.00

Taming Leviathan
Waging the War of Ideas Around the World
Edited by Colleen Dyble
Occasional Paper 142; ISBN 978 0 255 36607 6; £12.50

The Legal Foundations of Free Markets
Edited by Stephen F. Copp
Hobart Paperback 36; ISBN 978 0 255 36591 8; £15.00

Climate Change Policy: Challenging the Activists
Edited by Colin Robinson
Readings 62; ISBN 978 0 255 36595 6; £10.00

Should We Mind the Gap?
Gender Pay Differentials and Public Policy
J. R. Shackleton
Hobart Paper 164; ISBN 978 0 255 36604 5; £10.00

Pension Provision: Government Failure Around the World
Edited by Philip Booth et al.
Readings 63; ISBN 978 0 255 36602 1; £15.00

New Europe's Old Regions
Piotr Zientara
Hobart Paper 165; ISBN 978 0 255 36617 5; £12.50

Central Banking in a Free Society
Tim Congdon
Hobart Paper 166; ISBN 978 0 255 36623 6; £12.50

Verdict on the Crash: Causes and Policy Implications
Edited by Philip Booth
Hobart Paperback 37; ISBN 978 0 255 36635 9; £12.50

The European Institutions as an Interest Group
The Dynamics of Ever-Closer Union
Roland Vaubel
Hobart Paper 167; ISBN 978 0 255 36634 2; £10.00

Other IEA publications

Comprehensive information on other publications and the wider work of the IEA can be found at www.iea.org.uk. To order any publication please see below.

Personal customers

Orders from personal customers should be directed to the IEA:
Bob Layson
IEA
2 Lord North Street
FREEPOST LON10168
London SW1P 3YZ
Tel: 020 7799 8909. Fax: 020 7799 2137
Email: blayson@iea.org.uk

Trade customers

All orders from the book trade should be directed to the IEA's distributor:
Gazelle Book Services Ltd (IEA Orders)
FREEPOST RLYS-EAHU-YSCZ
White Cross Mills
Hightown
Lancaster LA1 4XS
Tel: 01524 68765, Fax: 01524 53232
Email: sales@gazellebooks.co.uk

IEA subscriptions

The IEA also offers a subscription service to its publications. For a single annual payment (currently £42.00 in the UK), subscribers receive every monograph the IEA publishes. For more information please contact:
Adam Myers
Subscriptions
IEA
2 Lord North Street
FREEPOST LON10168
London SW1P 3YZ
Tel: 020 7799 8920, Fax: 020 7799 2137
Email: amyers@iea.org.uk